The
Down-to-Earth Guide to
Global Warming

The
Down-to-Earth Guide to
Global Warming

Laurie David and Cambria Gordon

ORCHARD BOOKS • NEW YORK
AN IMPRINT OF SCHOLASTIC INC.

Library of Congress Cataloging-in-Publication Data

David, Laurie. Gordon, Cambria.

The Down-to-Earth Guide to Global Warming / by Laurie David and Cambria Gordon.

 p. cm.

ISBN-13: 978-0-439-02494-5
ISBN-10: 0-439-02494-3

1. Global warming—Juvenile literature. I. Gordon, Cambria. II. Title.

QC981.8.G56D38 2007

363.738'74—dc22

2006035705

10 9 8 7 6 5 4 3 2   07 08 09 10 11
Printed in the U.S.A.   03

First edition, September 2007

Book Design by Charles Kreloff

Text is printed on FSC–certified paper
that is 100% post-consumer waste.

Recycled
Supporting responsible use
of forest resources
www.fsc.org Cert no. SW-COC-2082
© 1996 Forest Stewardship Council

FSC

For Cazzie and Romy, so that they can finally understand what I have been talking about, and to the staff at the Natural Resources Defense Council — more than 300 lawyers, scientists, and policy experts who have devoted their lives to protecting our environment

— L. D.

For Micah, Arlo, and Capp, who keep me down to Earth, and for Laurie, who opened my eyes

— C. G.

Acknowledgments

They say that it takes a village to raise a child. Well, the authors believe that it also takes a village to write a children's book. We could not have completed this book without the help of so many. First and foremost, a thank-you to our husbands, Larry and Howard, who have supported our passion for the environment with both humor and love. Thank you to the experts at the Natural Resources Defense Council: Allen Hershkowitz, Andrew Wetzler, Darby Hoover, Jack Murphy, Jon Coifman, Kate Wing, Lisa Suatoni, Luke Tonachel, Nathanial Greene, and especially the ever-patient Dan Lashof, Joel Reynolds, John Steelman, and Tim Greeff for the extra time they put in to help us understand the complexities of global warming; Susan Hassol for her endless reads and thoughtful scientific assessments; Brendan DeMelle and Rachel Diamond, the best researchers any authors could ask for; Dawn Woollen and Sara Altshul for their superb attention to detail; Liana Schwarz for her unlimited knowledge, patience, and coordination of our fact-checking; Eric Wolff, Dr. Gareth Marshall, and the scientists at British Antarctic Survey; Heidi Cullen of the Weather Channel, for her grasp of wacky weather; Richard Fox of the Butterfly Conservation; Erica Levine of Community Energy, Inc.; David Zutler of Biota, for kindly responding to our inquiries; Cristina Mittermeier, Executive Director, International League of Conservation Photographers, for her willingness to lend images to this book ⬤.; and Dr. Mark Spencer, Director of the Environmental Leadership Opportunity Program College of Natural Resources UC Berkeley. Grateful acknowledgment is made to Reggie Bush, Cedric the Entertainer, Sheryl Crow, Leonardo DiCaprio, Jennifer Garner, Laird Hamilton, Jim Lovell, and Shaun White for their participation and insightful comments. Much appreciation goes to Judy Rothman for the impetus to do a cool kids' project on the environment; to Jennifer Jaeger at Andrea Brown Literary Agency for her undying belief in this book; Brian Lipson at Endeavor for his astute pro bono legal counsel; our gracious editor, Lisa Sandell, for her insightful comments, flag-waving enthusiasm, and vision; Amla Sanghvi, photo editor extraordinaire; Siobhán McGowan, for helping bring this book to fruition; and the incredible members of the Scholastic design team, Charles Kreloff, Kay Petronio, David Saylor, and Becky Terhune, who brought our vision to life.

Contents

3
Extinction Stinks

4
What You Can Do to Stop Global Warming

*****Boldface** indicates a term defined in the Words to Know section on page 100.

Authors' Note

Since this book was written, much has happened and breaking news stories about global warming are coming fast. Here are some big developments that we learned about right as we were going to press:

The United States Supreme Court ruled that carbon dioxide and other global warming emissions are indeed pollutants under the Clean Air Act, so the Environmental Protection Agency has the authority to start cutting them. This is good news for the planet!

The Intergovernmental Panel on Climate Change (IPCC), a group made up of hundreds of scientists from around the world, concluded in its latest report that the warming of the climate system is unequivocal and very likely due to human activity. The third installment of IPCC's four-part report echoes the Stern Report, issued in England, which concluded that the costs of stabilizing the planet are significant but manageable and that the longer we wait, the more costly and dangerous it will become.

Scientists at the National Ice and Snow Center of Colorado, using satellite data and visual confirmation, found the polar ice cap to be melting much faster — 30 years faster! — than the IPCC predicted.

"Noah's Ark," a recent study by researchers at Bologna's Institute for Atmospheric Sciences and Climate Change, has concluded that many famous historical monuments are at risk from climate change. Both drought and intense rains could threaten the marble, metal, and wood in such beloved European landmarks as the Greek Parthenon, the Eiffel Tower, the Roman Colosseum, and the Tower of London.

China is expected to surpass the United States as the number one source of global warming emissions in the next year or two.

A diverse group of corporations from around the world, including General Electric, Air France, Volvo, and Citigroup, have formed the Global Round Table on Climate Change. This nonpolitical coalition is asking its governments to set targets to reduce CO_2 emissions. Similarly, corporations in the United States, including General Motors, PepsiCo, Royal Dutch Shell's U.S. subsidiary, BP America, ConocoPhillips, and Johnson & Johnson, have formed the United States Climate Action Partnership. They are also asking Congress to limit greenhouse gas emissions. This is especially notable because many of these corporations are in the oil and gas business!

Australia and Canada have voted to ban the use of regular incandescent lightbulbs by 2009 and 2012, respectively.

The city of San Francisco voted to outlaw the use of plastic checkout bags in large supermarkets by Fall 2007 and in large chain pharmacies about six months after that. In the United States and Canada, some of the biggest retailers, including Home Depot, Wal-Mart, and Ikea, and sports complexes like Boston's Fenway Park, are taking steps to promote sustainable products and reduce the carbon footprint of their stores.

Former Vice President Al Gore and the IPCC were awarded the Nobel Peace Prize in October 2007 for their work to increase awareness of global warming.

The U.S. government is working on a law that would phase out regular lightbulbs over the next seven years. The European Union, Canada, and Australia are also planning phaseouts, and China is considering it as well.

As our Earth continues to show signs of global warming, people are showing signs of action. We salute you.

Dear Reader,

We are proud to present *The Down-to-Earth Guide to Global Warming*. This book was born out of our desire for kids to know the truth about this problem and what they can do to help solve it. The consequences of global warming are seen every day in extreme weather events, in the news media, and in our own backyards. It can be scary not understanding global warming, especially if we don't know how to be part of the effort to solve it. On a personal note, as moms, we have the responsibility to make sure that in the years to come, when we are asked by our own children, *what did you know, when did you know it, and what did you do?*, we are able to answer these questions.

   The Down-to-Earth Guide to Global Warming is divided into four parts. The first deals with the science of global warming and explains why it happens and how we arrived at our present situation. The second talks about the effect global warming is having on our weather systems. The third part focuses on global warming's impact on plant and animal life, while the final section covers, among other things, the many steps kids, along with their parents, teachers, and friends, can take to help reverse this problem.

   There has never been a more important time to talk about global warming and to take action. Every person on this planet, young or old, has a part to play. By reading this book and giving it to others to read, you're becoming a part of the solution, too.

We hope this book will inspire you to help stop global warming!

Sincerely,

Laurie David   *Cambria Gordon*

Laurie David and Cambria Gordon
Los Angeles, California, 2007

The
Down-to-Earth Guide to
Global Warming

Part 1
It's Getting Hot in Here

So What Exactly *Is* Global Warming?

Picture this: It's late at night. You're asleep in bed, with lots of blankets covering you. Suddenly, you wake up all hot and sweaty, so you kick off the covers. Cool air hits your legs. Much better. You fall back to sleep and wake up refreshed, ready for school.

Now picture the Earth. Certain gases that have been collecting in the atmosphere for the past 100 years are creating a heavy blanket around the Earth. **Heat from the sun gets trapped under the blanket and the Earth begins to feel too hot. But the Earth can't just kick off that cover to cool down. This is global warming.**

Of all the gases in the atmosphere, carbon dioxide (CO_2) contributes the most to global warming. But CO_2 is also necessary to sustain life. CO_2 is released into the atmosphere when dead organisms decompose and volcanoes erupt. It is then absorbed by plants, which use it to grow, and by the oceans, which use it to nourish sea life, beginning with microscopic plants called algae.

Our planet is heating up.

Humans and other animals eat plants and exhale carbon dioxide when they breathe, completing the cycle. And over thousands and millions of years, much of this carbon ends up buried underground or at the bottom of the oceans.

Every living thing on planet Earth is part of the natural carbon cycle.

This is how it has always worked. But, recently, we have been asking too much of the carbon cycle. **Cars, factories, and electric power plants have been putting too much of this buried carbon into our atmosphere.**

You might be thinking, why is global warming so important now? Well, because the Earth is the only home we have. When weather patterns are altered, life as we know it will be altered, too. We'll feel the changes every season of the year, while at home or on vacation. For example, global warming is causing some summer nights to be as warm as summer days, preventing people's bodies from getting a necessary break from the heat, and this creates serious health risks. Global warming is also causing less snow to fall in the higher altitudes, so your favorite ski and snowboard spot might be closed when you get there.

Global warming is a problem that's happening now. The good news is that we still have time to solve it.

While the Earth is indeed good at absorbing carbon dioxide, it can only handle so much. If carbon dioxide were a pizza, then we are expecting the Earth to eat a whole pie rather than just one slice. In other words, we're releasing too much carbon dioxide, too fast.

A Greenhouse Gas Is Not Caused by an Orchid Grower Who Ate Too Many Beans

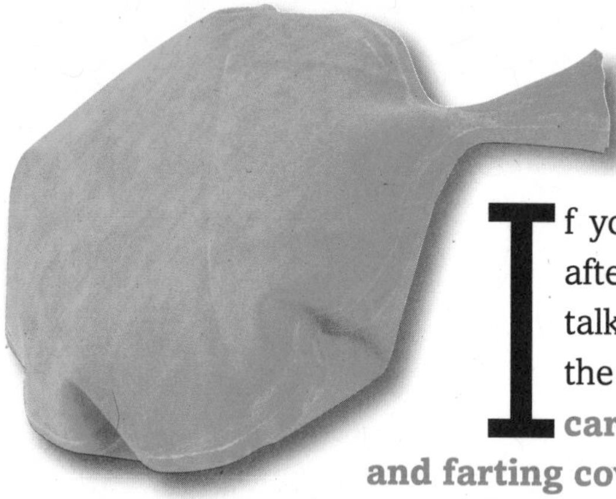

That would be gas in the greenhouse.

I f you've ever eaten too many burritos, then you know what can happen afterward. But we're not talking about that kind of gas. The gases we're talking about have been floating around in our atmosphere, surrounding the Earth, since life first began. **Greenhouse gases have names like carbon dioxide, methane (which, now that you mention it, burping and farting cows actually help produce), water vapor, nitrous oxide, and more.**

The reason they're called greenhouse gases is because they act just like a real glass-covered greenhouse, like the kind you could grow orchids in — or even beans. Both glass-covered greenhouses and greenhouse gases let sunlight in but prevent the warmth from escaping back out.

What Kinds of Greenhouse Gases Are In Our Air?

Carbon Dioxide 82%

Methane 9%

Nitrous Oxide 5%

Other 4%

Ever wonder where some of that methane comes from?

A little bit of greenhouse gas is good. It keeps our planet at a comfortable 57°F (14°C), a temperature that's averaged over the whole planet and across all the seasons. But at this point in history, we humans have released so much greenhouse gas into the atmosphere, the Earth's average temperature has actually risen one degree! Maybe you're thinking that doesn't sound so bad.

If the Earth's average temperature increases even a few degrees, gigantic changes can happen:

- Glaciers will melt.
- Oceans will get too warm, causing fiercer hurricanes.
- Animals and plants might die because they can't adapt to the change in temperature.
- And humans can suffer, too.

Too bad the Earth can't just stop eating burritos.

Consider this:

You know that Popsicle in your freezer? At 32°F (0°C), it freezes and stays solid enough for you to bite it. But at 33°F (0.5°C), it falls off the stick.

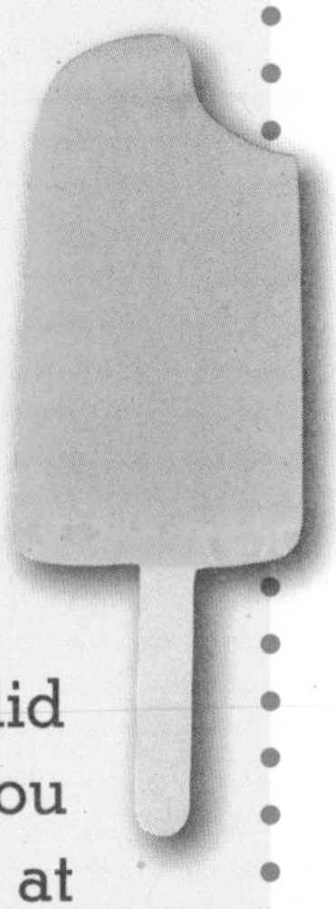

The Greenhouse Effect

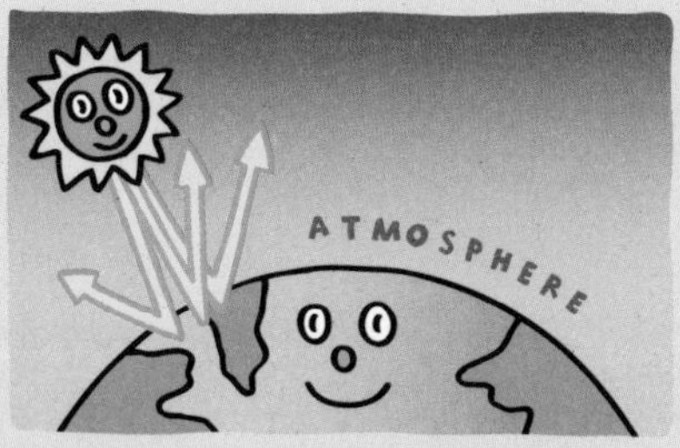

Normal Greenhouse Effect

When direct sunlight (**short-wave energy**) heads toward Earth, it passes right through greenhouse gases. Some of the sunlight is reflected by the clouds back into space, but most is absorbed by the Earth and is used to warm the planet's surface. The Earth then radiates some of that heat (**long-wave energy**) back into the atmosphere. Only then do greenhouse gases go to work, trapping long-wave energy and using it to keep the lower ten miles of our atmosphere livable.

Extreme Greenhouse Effect

With the increased amount of greenhouse gases in our atmosphere, too much long-wave energy is being trapped underneath the greenhouse blanket. The extra heat has nowhere to go but back down to Earth, warming the planet more than is healthy.

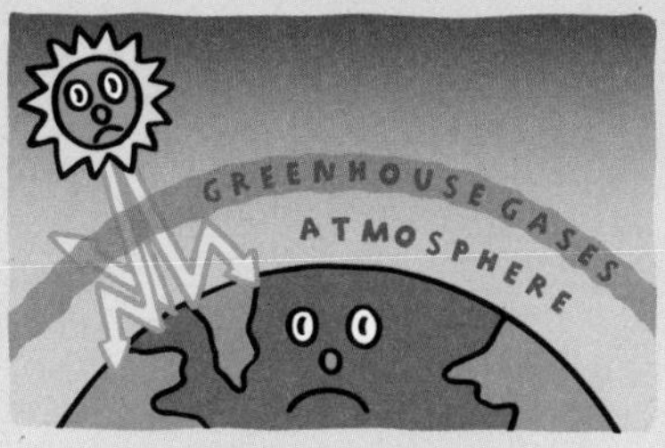

Were Fossil Fuels Once Dinosaurs?

If you've ever gone fossil hunting, then you know the thrill of finding a sea-snail shell or a rock with a leaf print embedded in it from millions of years ago. Well, what if you went fossil hunting and found a piece of coal? Or a drop of black oil? Even though it's highly unlikely, it's possible, because coal, oil, and natural gas were buried deep in the ground around the time of the dinosaurs. That's why they're called **fossil fuels**. But before we get ahead of ourselves, let's start at the beginning.

More than 300 million years ago, even before dinosaurs roamed the Earth, the land was covered with large trees, leafy plants, swamps, and oceans. In the water lived algae — tiny sea creatures ranging in size from a single cell to many cells. As our bodies need fat and carbohydrates for energy and growth, so do algae. We get our energy from the food we eat; algae get it from the sun. Algae use sunlight to convert carbon dioxide into carbohydrates, storing energy for growth. But they also store something else. Oil. **A microscopic amount of oil is present in all algae!**

When the prehistoric algae died, as all living things eventually do, they sank to the bottom of the water. They were then buried, either by sea or by **sediment**, which is a mishmash of sand, clay, and other minerals. Maybe an earthquake shook the ground so hard that sediment eventually covered an entire swamp, or an ice age came along suddenly and froze an ocean for thousands of years. However it happened, the algae lay there, buried.

Now, three miles (5 km) of seawater or dirt over your microscopic head can get pretty heavy. It can get hot, too.

The deeper you go toward the center of the Earth, as you approach what's called the mantle, the hotter it gets.

Also, heat is always released when dead matter decomposes. Well, it got very hot around all those dead algae, like an oven of sorts. And through time, this heat, along with the weight of the water and sediment, put pressure on the dead algae and squeezed it like your brother might squeeze your arm. This squeezing forced out the stored fat and carbohydrates from the algae, as well as the oil that was already there, and trapped it underground, where it turned into the black stuff — petroleum — that we use today to power our cars.

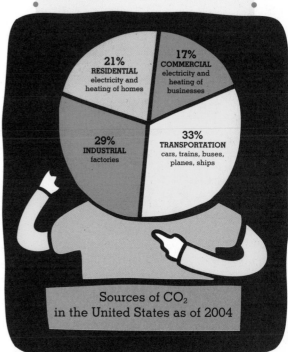

Where does all this CO_2 come from?

21% RESIDENTIAL electricity and heating of homes

17% COMMERCIAL electricity and heating of businesses

29% INDUSTRIAL factories

33% TRANSPORTATION cars, trains, buses, planes, ships

Sources of CO_2 in the United States as of 2004

Coal and natural gas, our two other fossil fuels, have slightly different origins. Coal started out as fallen forest trees and plant material that, over time, were also buried. Just like the energy that was forced out of the algae, heat and pressure forced water out from the dead plant material, leaving only a carbohydrate-filled mixture that looked a lot like dark paste, called peat. Over millions of years, the peat hardened into coal. Today, coal is mainly used to provide electricity.

Natural gas, or methane, originates from dead swamp matter that decomposed deeper down in the Earth than its oil counterpart. So deep, in fact, that no oxygen was present. (Oil is usually found closer to the Earth's surface than natural gas.) Chemicals like carbon and hydrogen were also squeezed out of the dead swamp matter, and the high heat and lack of oxygen caused a chemical reaction, changing the energy stored in the dead organic matter into natural gas. Today, natural gas is used to heat our homes and light our stoves.

It took millions of years for the three types of fossil fuels — oil, coal, and natural gas — to form, but humans have taken them out of the ground in a fraction of the time! And this is precisely where global warming fits in. All those prehistoric algae, plants, and dead matter were storing energy in the form of carbon. And what happens when you burn a fossil fuel? Its carbon combines with oxygen to become carbon dioxide, which is then released into the atmosphere.

The burning of fossil fuels is the biggest contributor to greenhouse gases and, therefore, the biggest contributor to global warming. And we do a lot of burning on this planet.

So the answer to the question at the start of this chapter is yes, today's oil, coal, and natural gas were once prehistoric algae, plants, and maybe some skin cells from a *Tyrannosaurus rex*. But the thing that makes fossil fuels truly like dinosaurs is that, with all the new, cleaner technologies people are beginning to discover and use, our dependence on dirty fossil fuels should become a thing of the past — and stay there.

A miner in Colorado extracts coal that will be burned later at a power plant.

You Say You Want a Revolution?

Revolution is an enormous change that occurs in history. People may fight against their leaders to change their governments. Or, on a smaller scale, if you wanted to have french fries in the cafeteria instead of broccoli, then you could try revolting. (A peaceful protest works wonders.) A revolution doesn't always have to occur by force. It can also happen because people make great changes in the way they do things. This happened in Great Britain in the 1750s, when the Industrial Revolution began.

Before the middle of the 1700s, people made most things by hand. Take that shirt you're wearing, for example. If you lived in the countryside of England in 1740, you probably used your fingers to comb the wool fibers that were sheared off a sheep. Once the fibers were all parallel and untangled, you then spun or twisted them, and threaded them onto a loom to make the cloth. This whole process took almost a week! But, in 1786, a man named Edmund Cartwright figured out a way to make a power loom that could do all that work in a matter of hours! **Once people tasted the sweet life of speed and efficiency, they didn't want to go back to doing things by hand again.**

By the mid-1800s, the Industrial Revolution had spread to North America, Japan, and beyond. It was an exciting

It's time for a new *clean, green* industrial revolution.

time, filled with a sense that anything was possible. Innovation and creativity popped up in unexpected places. A poor man could become a millionaire: All it took was one great idea. Steam engines powered the trains that crisscrossed the United States and revolutionized travel and shipping. Automobiles came next, with their internal combustion engines. Then Thomas Edison invented the first incandescent lightbulb, bringing electricity into the home. Electric power plants sprang up all over, burning coal to boil water into steam that would power the generators. Industry made people's lives easier. Millions of jobs were created and people prospered.

Nobody knew back then that all this industrial progress would end up changing the natural patterns of our climate. In fact, many scientists believe the Industrial Revolution was actually the start of global warming, because that's when we began burning fossil fuels in large quantities. *Now* **we know.**

Knowing doesn't mean you have to give up that shirt on your back or your ride to the mall or your reading light. Knowing doesn't mean the end of modern conveniences. And it certainly doesn't mean the end of jobs and prosperity. In fact, it's just the opposite. Knowing means a change in thinking that lets us power our lives differently.

What Is Green?

Besides the color you turn after riding a roller coaster ten times in a row, **green** traditionally represents nature and the richness of life on our planet. This is certainly one reason why the word has been adopted to describe everything that seeks to protect and preserve the well-being of people and the planet — from politics to products in your grocery store.

11

CO$_2$: The Big Kahuna

The year was 1958. In Hawaii, while most people were catching waves, a young scientist named Charles David Keeling climbed to the top of Mauna Loa, a mountain volcano high above the surf. There he planted a manometer, a device he invented to measure the gnarliest greenhouse gas of all: carbon dioxide. For one year, Keeling took a daily measurement of CO$_2$ concentration in the atmosphere. When he graphed his measurements, Keeling found that in the summer, carbon dioxide levels dipped down low because there were so many trees and plants that bloomed in the spring. All those extra leaves did just what they were supposed to: take CO$_2$ from the atmosphere and combine it with sunlight and a green pigment called chlorophyll to give themselves energy (aka photosynthesis).

The Keeling Curve

The Keeling Curve illustrates the concentration of CO_2 in the atmosphere, measured atop Mauna Loa, Hawaii, 1958–2005.

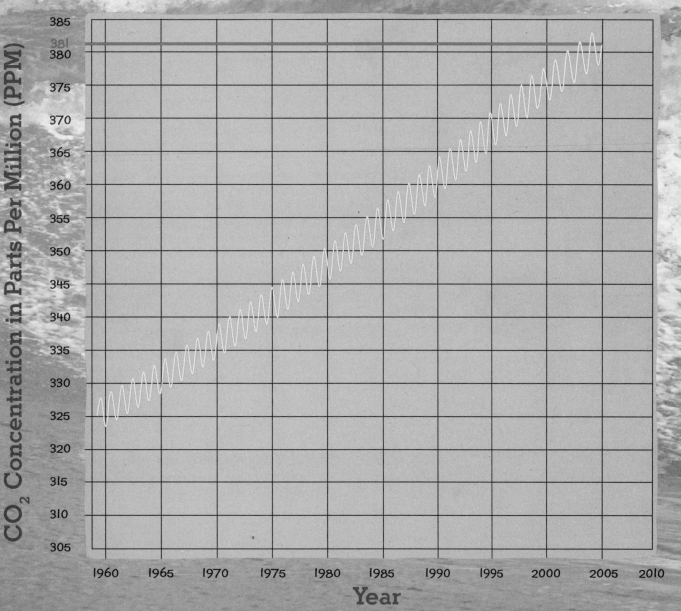

In the winter months, when the plants and trees shed their leaves, CO_2 levels increased because there was not as much photosynthesis going on, which means a lot less CO_2 was being consumed. Nature was doing its job.

The seasons were turning and the trees and plants were reacting perfectly. Keeling was so fascinated by these seasonal reflections of CO_2 concentrations that he continued taking measurements for three decades. It wasn't long before Keeling noticed something radical. The angle of the graph kept going up. The wintertime highs of CO_2 concentrations were getting higher and the summertime lows were not dipping down as low.

The amount of CO_2 in the Earth's atmosphere was rising every year.

What a discovery! The Keeling Curve became a famous image and is now accepted by scientists and surfers all over the world. Kowabunga.

How in the World Does Photosynthesis Work?

Photosynthesis is the way in which plants create food for themselves. Using a green pigment called chlorophyll, plants take energy from the sun and combine it with CO_2 and water to make sugar, which in turn gives them sustenance. The plants then release oxygen as a by-product. In other words, plants are keeping the carbon, but releasing the dioxide!

Fact: One tree can absorb the amount of CO_2 released by an average car that's been driven for 4,000 miles (6,437 km).

The Mystery of the Dome C Ice Core

The scientists from the British Antarctic Survey (BAS) are real-life sleuths who have uncovered clues to what weather was like hundreds of thousands of years ago. Wearing bear-paws (gloves) and mukluks (boots), they battle temperatures 40°F below zero (-40°C) in the harshest climate on Earth. In 2004, the folks from BAS drilled into the East Antarctica ice, at a spot called Dome C. Using a drill just four inches (10 cm) wide, they ground their way downward, separating a skinny column of ice and drawing it toward the surface. When they were done, they had gone more than two miles (3 km) down into the ice. That column of ice, called an ice core, dated back 650,000 years in time!

After studying the ice core, the scientists from BAS learned something startling. The amount of CO_2 in our atmosphere today is 27 percent higher than it was in their samples of ancient atmosphere. And it's rising faster and faster. Inside the Dome C ice core, a slow increase in CO_2 took place over a thousand years, where it took us modern-day humans just 17 years to cause the same kind of increase.

An overview of the British Antarctic Survey camp at Dome C.

CO$_2$ and Temperature

They Go Together Like Peanut Butter and Jelly. Milk and Cookies. Macaroni and Cheese. You Get the Picture.

After young Mr. Keeling figured out how to measure CO$_2$ concentrations in the atmosphere during the 1950s and '60s, scientists posed the question: What if we could measure CO$_2$ in the atmosphere from thousands of years ago? You're probably thinking that's impossible — time travel only happens in books or in the movies. But Antarctica is like a time machine if you're a glaciologist.

Scientists discovered that carbon dioxide and Antarctic temperature have gone hand-in-hand for 650,000 years!

Scientists of the British Antarctic Survey examine an ice core at Dome C in Antarctica.

Deep down in the Antarctic ice are atmosphere samples from the past, trapped in tiny air bubbles. These bubbles, formed when snowflakes fell on the ice, are the key to figuring out two things about climate history: what the temperatures were in the past and which greenhouse gases were present in the atmosphere at that time.

The more carbon dioxide in the atmosphere, the higher the temperature climbed.

The less carbon dioxide in the atmosphere, the lower the temperature fell. You can see this relationship for yourself by looking at the graph on your left, which actually combines measurements from three different places in Antarctica.

What makes this graph so amazing is that by connecting rising CO$_2$ to rising temperature, scientists have discovered the link between greenhouse gas pollution and global warming.

Remember that one-degree temperature rise we talked about earlier? Well, the Earth's average temperature has climbed from 57°F to 58°F (13.9°C to 14.4°C) in *less than 100 years*. We're warming up the planet faster than at any other time in history, and even the best detective in the world can't predict how much warmer it will get or how quickly that will happen.

I'm Melting!

I f the **polar ice caps** could speak, they'd sound just like the Wicked Witch of the West. Over the past 50 years, the average temperature on Earth has steadily increased, and it just keeps on climbing. While it's true that natural warming periods have occurred since life first began, what's happening in the present is a much more rapid warming. Eleven out of 12 of the years between 1994 and 2006 were the hottest on record. And July 2005 to June 2006 was the hottest 12-month period in the continental United States since we started measuring temperature! This extra heat is melting the ice at both poles, the polar ice cap in the north, and Antarctica in the south.

What happens at both ends of the Earth gives scientists a clue as to what will happen later to the middle of the planet.

Where Do Icebergs Come From?

An ice shelf is an extension into the ocean of glaciers or ice sheets that cover land. It's attached to the glacier by a kind of ice tether. Icebergs are born when outlying pieces of the shelf break off their tether due to the natural warming of the air and waters in summertime. The process is called calving, but no cows are involved whatsoever.

Here's why this is a big deal. In the same way your mom knows when you're getting sick even before you do, scientists know that melting poles are the first symptoms of an unhealthy Earth. Remember that one-degree temperature change we can't stop talking about? **Well, one degree hotter for the world on average is actually about two degrees hotter at the North Pole and slightly less than two at the South Pole.**

Take the Larsen B ice shelf. This is a block of ice in the Antarctic that has been frozen solid since the last ice age, for at least 11,500 years. In 2002, a chunk bigger than the state of Rhode Island collapsed into the sea, breaking into pieces. British and Belgian scientists found evidence that global warming played a role in bringing warmer air to the ice shelf. Warm, westerly winds, part of the **circumpolar** wind cycle that normally blows clockwise around the Antarctic peninsula, became so strong that they were able to get over a barrier of mountains that normally shield the Larsen B ice shelf. Winds that can cross mountains? **Pretty scary.**

A satellite view of the polar ice cap in 2003. The pink outline shows the boundaries of the ice cap in 1979. Can you see how much has melted?

In the year 2000, the largest single block of ice, the Ward Hunt ice shelf, started cracking. By 2002, it had split all the way through and is now breaking up into pieces. Even more recently, an ice cap the size of 33,000 basketball courts broke off from a Canadian arctic shelf. This has astounded scientists because it happened faster than they thought possible.

Without our polar ice caps, we don't have a natural cooling system for the Earth. Like an air conditioner cools down a house or car, our polar ice caps keep our planet cool by forming a white protective coating that reflects some of the sun's rays back into space; the fancy name for this process is the **albedo effect**. With smaller white ice caps, we have more blue sea and brown earth, surfaces that soak up heat, rather than reflect it. So melting ice caps actually speed up global warming. **Now that's wicked.**

Semipermanent?

Permafrost is rock or soil that has been frozen continuously for two or more years. In some places on Earth, it is more than 1,000 inches (2,540 cm) thick. Global warming is causing the permafrost to thaw in Siberia, which is surprising enough, because the word *perma* implies that it is permanently frozen. But

An aerial view of permafrost with ice wedge polygon patterns, taken in the arctic near Hope Bay, Nunavut, Canada.

what's even more surprising is what was found hiding in the permafrost. Methane gas, safely stored deep inside the permafrost for centuries, is now bubbling up toward the surface and escaping. Though methane doesn't last as long in the atmosphere as carbon dioxide, it is still a powerful, heat-trapping greenhouse gas, and the more of it that gets into the atmosphere, the more it will speed up global warming.

The Bald and the Beautiful

Our forests need trees. There's nothing beautiful about a bald forest. So how does a forest go bald and how does that contribute to global warming?

Let's go back to basics for a moment. Every breath we and other animals inhale contains oxygen. Every breath we exhale contains carbon dioxide. Trees and other plants absorb our carbon dioxide and convert it back into oxygen. This is how most living things stay alive.

But huge forests do more than just absorb the carbon dioxide that animals and humans breathe out. They absorb CO_2 from all over the world, whether it's released naturally from a volcano erupting in the South Pacific, by dead matter decomposing in India, or by forest fires raging on the West Coast of the United States — or whether it's released unnaturally, from burning fossil fuels.

A clear-cut mountain in Canada.

Every two seconds, a forest area the size of a football field is destroyed.

Forests help keep our atmosphere in balance by literally taking carbon dioxide out of the atmosphere and converting it back to carbon in leaves and roots, and in the soils below. Something that is not a source of carbon but that removes it from the equation by storing it, so to speak, is called a **carbon sink**. Over 40 years, one acre of newly planted forest will store 50 tons (45 metric tons) of carbon dioxide.

With more and more people living on Earth — 6.6 billion, to be exact — the demand for wood grows. We need it to build new homes, you use paper for school reports, and farmers want the forestry land to grow crops or let cattle graze, while developers use it to put up shopping malls. **Ancient forests once covered huge portions of the Earth, but we have already cut, burned, or cleared 80 percent of our original primary forests!** To give you an idea of how big that is, think of your body as a forest: the length from the top of your head to just below your knees is 80 percent.

When entire forests are chopped down or burned, this is called **clear-cutting**. Clear-cutting is bad for two reasons: 1) It leaves fewer trees out there to absorb carbon dioxide and 2) it smashes open the piggy bank, releasing large amounts of carbon dioxide into the air that, for centuries, have been safely tucked deep in the roots and soil of the forests. Deforestation is the second-largest contributor to global warming after the burning of fossil fuels.

Remember the CO_2 and temperature graph? The more CO_2 in the air, the more the planet warms up. The more the planet warms up, the drier the soil and trees become. The more dried-out the soil and trees are, the higher the chance of devastating forest fires. When lightning or meteorites strike a dried-out forest, it can go up in flames much faster than a healthy forest. In the United States, the fire season has become two months longer. Fires are now fiercer, harder to put out, and therefore burn longer. **The worst and most expensive wildfire season in the history of the United States occurred in 2006.**

In the case of forests, bald is definitely *not* beautiful.

CO_2 works sort of like perfume. If you open up a perfume bottle in the middle of the room, eventually the smell reaches every corner. Similarly, CO_2 reaches every corner of the globe.

Don't Break the Bank

If you're asking yourself what in the world a carbon sink is, this might help: Forests and soils store carbon dioxide like your piggy bank stores money. When you cut down a forest, it's just like smashing your piggy bank. But there's one difference: Carbon dioxide can't buy you anything good.

The Oceans Are Carbon Sponges

Everything is connected!

Some people study global warming by separating the planet into three parts: 1) the air, 2) the land, and 3) the sea. But when it comes to CO_2, all three parts are in fact connected, and if something happens in one of the parts, the other two are affected. The planet is kind of like a group of friends. Say one friend wins the lottery. Suddenly every friend or classmate he never knew existed will appear on his doorstep with a smile and a plate of cookies. You can't make one friend rich and hope that the others won't notice. Well, you can't put that much CO_2 into the air and hope the land and sea won't notice.

When there is too much CO_2 in the air, the sea takes up the slack, soaking up the extra CO_2 like a gigantic sponge. The oceans have been doing this since the Earth was first formed. It is part of the oceans' job to keep the planet's CO_2 levels in balance, or **equilibrium**. The problem now is that with so much CO_2 in our atmosphere from burning fossil fuels, the oceans, like our air, are getting warmer.

Everything is connected *inside* the oceans, too. Surface water is connected to deep water by ocean currents. The waters need to mix together to keep nutrients moving around. But warmer surface waters don't mix well with colder deep waters. It has to do not only with temperature, but also with density — meaning how much salt and other minerals are present and how heavy that makes the water. Polar ice melt is dumping freshwater into the ocean and reducing the salt content of the surface waters, making them lighter. When ocean waters have different temperatures and densities, **stratification** occurs, which is similar to what happens with oil and vinegar in your salad dressing bottle. They don't mix: The heavier oil stays on the bottom, while the lighter vinegar sits above it. And we can't just shake up the oceans to mix up the layers.

This warmer water/stratification thing isn't good for plankton, the microscopic plants that are the basis for all ocean life. And believe us when we say that we don't want plankton to be endangered. Every fish in the sea depends on plankton, whether it eats plankton directly or eats a smaller fish that does, and many humans and animals depend on fish as one of their main food sources.

There's one other important fact about global warming and oceans. *Cold* seawater absorbs more carbon dioxide than *warm* seawater. **If CO_2 emissions continue to rise, the oceans will simply be too warm to take up as much CO_2 as they have been.** In other words, they will be less able to act like the happy sponges they want to be and more CO_2 will be stuck in our atmosphere.

What's the Deal with Plankton?

Plankton live on the surface of the ocean, soaking up sunlight and carbon dioxide from the atmosphere just like — you guessed it — a sponge. Plankton feed on nutrients like tasty nitrogen and phosphorus from deep down in the cold waters. But with stratification, there is less mixing of surface and deep water, so those nutrients stay at the bottom and the plankton don't reproduce. This affects not only what the fish eat but also, indirectly, global warming. When the plankton die naturally, they float down to the bottom of the sea and stay there, keeping the CO_2 they took out of the atmosphere safely stored for thousands of years. (Just like the algae from prehistoric times!) But if they don't reproduce, there go our carbon dioxide eaters, leaving more CO_2 in the atmosphere, which warms the planet even more. It's what we call a vicious cycle.

What Is Your Carbon Footprint?

Here's what it's not: when you stick your foot in a bucket of oil and step on a white rug. Here's what it is: the amount of carbon dioxide pollution that is emitted from the energy you use. Every year, each of us releases literally tons of carbon dioxide into the air. CO_2 is measured in pounds, and there are 2,000 lb (907 kg) in a ton. The average American adult emits 20 tons (18 metric tons) or 40,000 lb (18,144 kg) of CO_2 a year. And together, all human beings the world over add 100 million *tons* (91 million metric tons) of CO_2 into the atmosphere each day!

Your **carbon footprint** comes from normal, everyday activities like using your computer, turning on the light in your bedroom, taking a bath (heating water uses energy!), and riding in a bus or car to school. So let's take a moment and do some simple math to calculate your carbon footprint. Don't worry, you won't get graded on it. **But we hope you'll start to make the connection between how you live and your personal daily contribution to global warming.**

There is a number that represents how much CO_2 the atmosphere can hold before the harmful effects of global warming become unstoppable. It's an amount that scientists call the carbon budget. Every pound of carbon dioxide we put into the atmosphere is bringing us closer to reaching the limits of our budget.

Here are some average statistics for the average kid on an average day:

- Using a screen saver on the computer (based on an LCD monitor) emits 2.5 lb (1.1 kg) of carbon dioxide.

- Turning on the lights (based on three 60-watt bulbs in a ceiling fixture kept on for six hours a day) will generate 1.5 lb (680 g) of carbon dioxide.

- Taking a bath uses up to 3.5 lb (1.6 kg) of carbon dioxide. (Hint: Taking a two-minute shower is better!)

- Riding in a car to school uses 5 lb (2.3 kg) of CO_2 (based on driving to school 2.5 miles (4 km) each way in a car that gets 20 miles (32 km) per gallon).

Total = 12.5 lb (5.7 kg) of carbon dioxide per day

Now, if you take your daily number and multiply that by the number of kids between the ages of eight and 16 in the whole world, which is about 1.2 billion (that number looks like this: 1,200,000,000), that's more than 15.24 *billion* lb (6.9 billion kg) of

carbon dioxide per day! The Earth can handle only so much carbon.

Think about your bedroom closet. You fill it with clothes, shoes, board games, sports equipment, books, old toys, and suitcases. You can keep putting stuff in there, but there's a point at which the closet will be full. After that, put one more thing in there, even if it's something as small as a tennis ball, and everything will come toppling down on your head.

Every pound of CO_2 takes up space in the atmosphere. That's why it's so important to conserve energy. We don't want to use up our carbon budget. Luckily, there are lots of simple ways we can reduce our carbon footprints right away.

The Day After Tomorrow

Because CO_2 stays in the atmosphere for decades or more, almost half of the CO_2 you put in the atmosphere today will still be there when your grandchildren are born. This is why the problem of global warming is so urgent. Everything we do today means that we, and our families, are going to be living with the consequences tomorrow. We need to make a change and do things better.

Says Who?

Match the quote with the person who said it.

1 "The gases in the air soak up the sun's rays and then they're trapped. The heat keeps warmin' up the Earth. We keep getting hotter. We're like a big bag of microwave popcorn in here, people. Eventually, we're all gonna start poppin'!"

2 "I feel more at home in the sea than any other place on the planet. I want to help stop global warming because I want to protect my home. I know we can make a difference one by one."

3 "When I circled the moon and looked back at Earth, my outlook on life and my viewpoint of Earth changed. You don't see Las Vegas, Boston, or even New York. You don't see boundaries or people. When viewed in total, Earth is a spaceship just like Apollo. We are all the crew of Spaceship Earth; and just like Apollo, the crew must learn to live and work together. We must learn to manage the resources of this world with new imagination. The future is up to you."

4 "We can vote for leaders who care about protecting your health, air, and environment. We can support nonprofits who are making a difference. We can be environmentalists. So get educated. Stay educated. So we can think for ourselves. And join the fight to save this unique blue planet for future generations."

5 "Snow levels and global warming affect everyone, from snowboarders to accountants. We all need to take steps toward making sure we have a clean and healthy planet. Using fuel-efficient cars, recycling, and taking the time to spread the word are all great starts toward a better future."

6 "I have been so fortunate to have been adopted by the city of New Orleans in my first year with the Saints, and so I have witnessed global warming's impact from Hurricane Katrina firsthand. I have seen the wreckage and destruction, but I have also seen the resilience of the people who live here, and the proud looks on their faces as they rebuild. Kids have seen their playing fields torn to pieces, so we are working together to provide these children with new green fields to play on like I was lucky enough to have. Every kid needs an environmentally friendly field to play on, pesticide-free grass to run on, and clean air to breath."

7 "We live on a beautiful planet, but the state of its health will be the deciding factor in our own health and longevity. We seem to forget that the Earth is a living **organism** and that when it dies, we die. As we watch our climate change radically, it is imperative that we change the way we treat our planet."

8 "Imagine a world without polar bears. Or penguins! Or angel fish. I cannot imagine children growing up in that kind of world. It is up to us to make sure the world stays colorful and full of diverse life. In order to protect fish and animals and birds, we have to take care of our planet. After all, don't these animals deserve a place on this Earth besides *Happy Feet* and *Finding Nemo*?"

1.G; 2.H; 3.E; 4.F; 5.C; 6.A; 7.D; 8.B

A Football Player Reggie Bush

B Actress Jennifer Garner

C Snowboarder Shaun White

D Singer Sheryl Crow

E Astronaut Jim Lovell

F Actor Leonardo DiCaprio

G Comedian Cedric The Entertainer

H Surfer Laird Hamilton

29

Part 2
Weird, Wacky Weather

Hurricanes Flex Their Muscles

Here's the thing about global warming and hurricanes. Global warming doesn't cause hurricanes. It just makes them stronger. *Much* stronger.

Hurricanes need lots of warm, moist air to form and a steady supply of it to keep them going. To understand where the warm, moist air comes from, picture a pot of boiling water on the stove. You're about to pour some tasty pasta into that pot when the phone rings. You talk to your friend for ten minutes, forgetting all about the boiling water. By the time you remember to check the pot, the water has almost disappeared! The hot water evaporated in the form of steam, which in turn warmed the air above the pot. Well, the same thing happens with the oceans. **As the sun heats the ocean surface and the water temperature rises, the warm water evaporates into the air.** The moisture, called **water vapor**, then stays in the air. Of course, an ocean can never evaporate entirely. It's too deep. But what does evaporate can certainly warm the air above it enough to change the weather significantly.

A satellite view of Hurricane Katrina.

Kicking Up a Storm

Surface waters need to be around 78°F (26°C) or greater for a tropical storm to turn into a hurricane. Hurricane Katrina started as a Category 1 hurricane and turned into a Category 5 hurricane during the four days it passed through the Gulf of Mexico in the summer of 2005. The Gulf waters had an abnormally high surface temperature of 87°F (31°C)!

Think about the size of the Earth's oceans compared to your tiny pot of water. Even if a small area of a typically warm ocean heats up, that's plenty of energy to strengthen an average hurricane and turn it into a monster. Add water vapor to a storm and you may as well be giving it steroids.

Category 1 Hurricane

5-foot (1.5-m) waves

74- to 95-mph (119- to 153-kph) winds

some tree and shrubbery damage

damages weak structures

Category 3 Hurricane

9- to 12-foot (2.7- to 3.6-m) waves

111- to 130-mph (178- to 209-kph) winds

strips trees of leaves

destroys mobile homes

Category 5 Hurricane

18-foot (5.5-m) waves

155-mph (249-kph) winds

few trees left standing

many buildings destroyed

Flooded!

Everyone loves stomping in a puddle. Water bursts out from its center, spraying your shoes and the bottoms of your pants. But you probably never think about how that puddle got there. Most likely, it rained suddenly and the water didn't have enough time to be absorbed into the ground. Well, imagine thousands of puddles and imagine them moving, pooling together, pouring into storm drains and swollen rivers that overflow. We're talking torrents of water, rushing down your street and through your front door — water that the ground couldn't absorb because it simply came down too hard and too fast for too long. **That, friends, is a flood.**

The weird thing about global warming is that it will cause harder, faster downpours in places that normally get light rain; in places that normally see huge snowfall, it will cause more rain and less snow.

Cows wading in a flooded pasture in Broward County, Florida, in 1999, after Hurricane Irene.

Heavier rainfall will be more frequent and lighter drizzles will be less frequent, so that in some areas on the planet, such as China, there will be flooding in one province and drought in the province right next to it. **But overall, rainfall is increasing over large parts of the world, especially the type of storm that brings a huge downpour in a short period of time. And with faster, heavier rain comes flooding.**

As global warming raises the Earth's temperature, more water evaporates from the ground, putting more water vapor into the air. (Just like the surface waters of the oceans!) Let's talk about the properties of water for a moment. Depending on the temperature of water and the temperature of the air around it, water can take on three forms: gas, liquid, or solid. From our boiling pot of pasta, we know that warm water becomes a gas — water vapor. But if we turn off the heat and put a lid on the pot, little drops of water form on the underside of the lid. The air above the pot has cooled off enough to change the gas back into a liquid. And we know that at 32°F (0°C), water freezes and becomes a solid — ice.

After that pot of water reaches the boiling point, the water temperature stays at 212°F (100°C). But if the water boils for, say, five minutes, where does all that heat from the stove go? It goes into the evaporated water!

Storm Watcher

There are many names for storms and it can get confusing, even for the experts. A monsoon is a seasonal rain that occurs when air from a hot landmass meets air from a cool ocean. More than half the globe is affected by monsoon season, which occurs from June through November, including parts of Asia, Africa, and North America. A typhoon is a tropical storm (warm air) just like a hurricane, but they are called typhoons in the Pacific Ocean, and hurricanes in the Atlantic.

Though floods have occurred throughout history, they haven't happened that frequently. Global warming is changing that.

A flooded farm in California.

That heat is called latent heat. Latent heat is hidden energy — in this case, hidden inside the water vapor. That energy can be released later, if the water changes its form. Okay, back to the weather.

High in the sky, as the temperature gets cooler, water vapor condenses, or changes, into little liquid droplets that look like mist. The mist stage is actually clouds. But these little droplets get bigger when there is increased water vapor present. Then, when there is so much liquid in the atmosphere that the air can't hold any more, the drops fall down as rain. So you can see the relationship between water vapor and rain. **The more water vapor in the atmosphere, the more latent heat. The more latent heat, the more energy to intensify the rain. The more intense the rain, the more flooding. And it all adds up to disaster.**

While it is true that some flooding is due to newly built roads, houses, and buildings that change, or erode, the natural pathways for water to run off the ground, between 1950 and 2000 there were more floods than in any recorded 50-year period. **In the year 2000, there were more natural disasters than in any other single year up to that time, and 23 percent of those were floods.** Even in Asia, where the population is used to monsoons and typhoons, there were more than 300 floods between the years 1990 and 2000. In August 2006, Typhoon Saomai, the strongest storm to hit China in more than 50 years, dumped more than 12 inches (30.5 cm) of rain in just 12 hours. One downpour in India, during the summer of 2005, brought 37 inches (94 cm) of rain in 24 hours! That's the first three steps of a ladder.

In some towns and cities, there are man-made defenses to prevent floods — channels, locks, levees, dams, canals, and storm drains. Sometimes they hold, sometimes they don't. Tragically, in New Orleans in 2005, during Hurricane Katrina, they did not.

Global warming is here. That means more intense rains are coming. **Better roll up your pants.**

Icky Water

Sometimes floodwaters take days or even weeks to recede. The pools of standing water become breeding grounds for disease-carrying mosquitoes and other bugs.

A Thirsty Planet

Most people are lucky enough to be able to go to the sink and get a drink of water when they're thirsty. Planet Earth isn't so lucky. Droughts are drying out the land, and the ground is simply not getting enough to drink.

We talked about how weird it is that global warming makes rainfall heavier in some places. But in others, there's no rain at all. This is bad news for farmers in the middle of the United States and in parts of Australia, India, and China. Little or no rain during the growing season might be great for an outdoor party, but it's terrible for the crops. And this does no one any good. Not the farmer. Not the salad eater.

So how else will you be affected by the droughts? Let's start with where your drinking water comes from. Depending on where you live, it can come from underground wells or from streams, lakes, and rivers. In many parts of the world, river and lake water starts out as snow on mountaintops. During spring and summer, winter snow melts, flows down the mountains into the streams, rivers, and lakes, and then is diverted to public water companies, which make it safe to drink and then pipe it into your home. Dams and reservoirs also collect rainwater, which is then purified for drinking by these same water companies. **But with warmer temperatures caused by global warming, more rain is falling on the mountaintops than snow. The rain runs off too rapidly and is lost as a source of drinking water.**

In 2001 the snowpack on Washington's Mount Rainier was very light, causing drought conditions and this riverbed to dry up.

A Moving Story

When drought happens, whole communities are sometimes forced to relocate because their land simply can't sustain them. This can cause fighting between populations, and may ultimately lead to war.

Map labels:
- South Dakota
- Wyoming
- California
- Arizona
- Nebraska
- NORTH AMERICA
- Minnesota
- Tennessee
- Alabama
- England
- EUROPE
- ASIA
- China
- Mauritania
- Mali
- Cape Verde
- Gambia
- Eritrea
- Ethiopia
- Sudan
- Afghanistan
- Djibouti
- Somalia
- Kenya
- AFRICA
- North Pacific Ocean
- North Atlantic Ocean
- SOUTH AMERICA
- South Atlantic Ocean
- South Pacific Ocean
- Indian Ocean
- AUSTRALIA
- Chile
- EQUATOR
- South Pacific Ocean
- Southern Ocean
- ANTARCTICA

How Dry We Are

Here are the areas of the world that were experiencing severe drought at the time this book went to press. Many more regions are experiencing moderate drought.

If you live in California, Arizona, or Colorado, you can blame the shrinking snowfall amounts for your drought problems. If you live in Perth, Australia, and use well water, you can blame the summer rain, which falls on bare fields, soaks down deep into the earth, and mixes with salty seawater, making it undrinkable. If you live in the Sudan on the continent of Africa, you can blame the warmer Indian Ocean, which prevents monsoons from building.

Some monsoons can be a welcome addition to a dry region. In fact, monsoons are the main source of rainwater for the Sudan, a very dry region of Africa. But unlike hurricanes that form from warmer oceans, monsoons cannot form if the ocean is *too* warm. **Monsoons need a pronounced temperature difference between hot land and cool ocean to start brewing, so if the ocean is too warm, the monsoon never materializes.**

There is another side effect of drought. **Droughts can dry up our land so much that they can literally change a forest into a desert.** Sometimes a forest can be brought back naturally, but this takes a lot of rain over hundreds of years. And sometimes the forest floor never recovers its nutrient-rich soil necessary for forest vegetation, and remains a dry wasteland forever.

A cornfield in Colorado has dried up and died due to extreme drought.

Heat Waves: The X-Games of Summer

I f you've ever watched extreme sports, then you know they're not like regular sports. They're scarier and more dangerous. Really, only a daredevil does triple flips on a dirt bike shooting 40 feet (12.2 m) in the air.

Just as extreme sports are sports taken to the extreme, global warming can take summer's heat to the extreme, too.

Kevin Robinson executing a Flair on the Mega Ramp at X-Games 12.

41

Heat Waves Affect Animals, Too

In the summer of 2006, in central California, hundreds of sheep died during a 10-day heat wave. Ranchers also lost cattle. Try fitting 5,000 cows into an air-conditioned barn.

CAPACITY 5000

Dogs suffering from heat exhaustion rest in the shade.

Fact: In the summer of 1995, Chicago experienced this type of heat wave and hundreds of people died. In the summer of 2003, in Europe, thousands of people died during another terrible heat wave.

Spectators at a German soccer game are sprayed with water to cool off, as Europe is battered by a record-breaking heat wave in the summer of 2003.

Our summer weather is already warm. **Global warming makes it worse**. Heat waves — a number of consecutive days of unusually high heat — occur because there is a pressure change in the atmosphere. This means that the amount of upper air pushing down on the Earth, the oceans, and the air below it increases. This increased air pressure, which is a little like having a defensive linebacker sitting on you, prevents the cooler jet stream (ocean) air from making it onto land. This is a phenomenon that has always been a part of our weather cycle. However, this situation is worsened by all the CO_2 that has built up in the atmosphere. **The increased heat throughout our planet's overall system, both in the air and on the land, can turn a typical one-week heat wave into three weeks.**

What's worse is when hot temperatures combine with increased humidity. We talked about how global warming can put more water vapor in the atmosphere. But increased water vapor in the air doesn't necessarily mean rain will follow. Remember, rain falls when the temperature drops enough to cause water vapor to condense into liquid. Sometimes, the air simply does not cool enough to form rain. In those situations, the dense, moist air (humidity) just sits there, so that 100°F (38°C) can actually feel like 120°F (49°C).

It's not just the heat during the day, either; it's the warmer nights. People need cooler nights to return their body temperatures to normal. Air-conditioning helps, but only half the homes in America have it; most of the homes in Europe do not. And what happens when energy use is too high and a blackout occurs? *All* the air conditioners stop working.

In 2006, in the United States, 2,300 heat records were broken in the month of July alone, and all 50 states had temperatures above their normal average. And 2007 is expected to be the world's warmest year yet.

There is one difference between the X-Games and global warming. **The X-Games are cool. Global warming is not.**

An abandoned house in Nags Head, Cape Hatteras, North Carolina, which loses 12 feet (3.5 m) of beach a year.

Beach Bummer

One billion people in the world live on or near a coast. Some are wealthy, living in sprawling homes, while some are poor, living in humble shacks. But global warming does not discriminate. All homes located in coastal areas will be affected by it. Not to mention the beautiful beaches where we play volleyball, fly kites, build sand castles, and surf.

It has to do with rising sea levels. In other words, the normal heights of calm seas will become higher. Already in the last 100 years, global sea levels have risen eight inches (20 cm). Half of it is due to global warming. As water warms, it expands and takes up more space. Ever try opening up a new jar of applesauce and the lid won't budge? If you run the jar lid under hot water, it's a lot easier to open. This is because the lid expands when it's warmer, too.

Another way sea levels rise is when land-based ice melts and runs into the sea. Ice is melting rapidly all over the planet, but climatologists are most worried about the Greenland ice sheet. Greenland is the world's largest island, and more than 80 percent of it is covered in ice. The people living there are settled on the narrow, rocky coast. It's hard to believe that ice two miles (3 km) deep and as wide as half of the

Fact: If the Greenland ice sheet melts completely, it will add enough water to raise sea levels all across the world by 21 feet (6.4 m)!

United States can melt, but it has already begun to.

Here's where the beaches come in. Twenty-one feet (6.4 m) is pretty tall. It's higher than three Shaquille O'Neals stacked up. All that water is going to eat away at existing coastlines. That means we will have to redraw the maps of the world because entire blocks of land that are now above sea level will be under the water.

Until now, we've talked about some pretty wacky weather. We know it can get confusing; it's as if the information is in conflict with itself. How can we have both flooding and drought? How can we have both hurricanes and heat waves? There might even be a season in which there is no weird weather and we might get comfortable and think global warming isn't really a problem. Here's a hint to help you make sense of it all: **Global warming causes extreme weather in different places.** It has to do with where a place is positioned on the planet. Because the Earth is a sphere, the area in the middle receives the sun's heat differently than the areas closer to the poles, which are tilted farther away from the sun. In fact, the closer you move to the equator, the more intense the sunlight. This difference in how different parts of the Earth heat up is what creates and drives our weather. All weather — wind, rain, snow, and clear skies — begins with the sun's heat. So depending on where you're standing, global warming will affect you differently. But trust us. **It *will* affect all of us.**

For the people of Tuvalu, Shishmaref, Miami, Los Angeles, and so many more beautiful beaches on Earth, the future could be a real bummer.

The ocean has crept up and covered the streets of Tuvalu.

Buried Treasures

Rising sea levels caused by global warming have already affected two beautiful land areas. The islanders on Tuvalu in the South Pacific have had to make plans for their eventual evacuation. When their island disappears, residents will move to New Zealand. And in Shishmaref, Alaska, where an Inuit village has existed for 4,000 years, the land has eroded so much that the people are being forced to move.

A Walk in the Park?

When people use the phrase "a walk in the park," they mean that something is easy. Later on in this book, we'll show you that reducing carbon dioxide is actually easier than you think. But here's something that's *not* a walk in the park: watching our national parks suffer because of global warming.

Some of our parks are named for their natural phenomena — Glacier National Park in Montana and Joshua Tree National Park in the deserts of southern California, for example. **But scientists are predicting that within 25 years, all the Montana glaciers will have melted, and that by the end of this century, almost all the Joshua trees will be gone.** People visit North Cascades National Park in Washington State to see the ice caves, but they, too, are melting. Yellowstone

A view of Mount Rainier National Park.

Our national parks contain natural treasures, as their names often suggest. We must all make sure there is never a place called Global Warming National Park.

National Park became even more well-known from a famous cartoon character from the 1970s called Yogi Bear, but today, grizzly bears at Yellowstone can't find food and are starving. The trees they depend on for much of their food — pine nuts and moths — are dying from an infestation of beetles that thrive in warmer weather. The Florida Everglades are losing mangrove trees, which protect the area from rising sea levels. If the growth of mangrove trees can't keep up with the increased seawater, the freshwater Everglades will disappear — and along with that, the plants and animals that live in this habitat. And there are many other national parks that are threatened with loss of wildlife, fishing, and just plain old "enjoying the view."

Backyard BBQ

Here's what can happen in your own backyard (or close by) as the globe starts to sizzle and CO_2 levels continue to rise.

Poison ivy grows larger and becomes itchier.

Urushiol (can you say it fast three times?) is the toxin that makes poison ivy itchy. The more carbon dioxide in the air, the more urushiol the plant produces.

Fall leaves turn a dull color and won't last as long.

Green leaves need at least one frost to trigger their color change to red. As summer heat lasts longer, sometimes through the fall months, frosts are delayed and the beautiful colors we've come to expect all over the northeastern United States are being threatened.

Ski seasons get shorter.

In some ski resorts in Oregon and Washington, there's simply too much rain and not enough snow to last a whole ski season. Did you know that the 2006 Winter Olympics in Italy had to make fake snow because there wasn't enough of the real stuff?

Allergies are triggered and asthma worsens.

Ragweed and pinecones produce much more pollen when carbon dioxide levels are higher.

Outdoor ice rinks shrink.

Ice skaters and hockey players in places like Wisconsin and Massachusetts are finding their outdoor sports are getting tougher to play, due to warmer winters that keep lakes from freezing completely and rinks from staying frozen.

Disease-carrying ticks and mosquitoes move up in the world.

As areas above the equator warm up, ticks and mosquitoes can now exist in northern places where they could not have before — bringing Lyme disease, malaria, West Nile Virus, dengue, and yellow fever from their former exotic homes.

Bark beetle population explodes.

Cold winters used to kill this pesky tree-eater, but with warmer weather, many species of trees are falling prey to them — trees that provide food for bears and other animals.

Pancakes get drier.

Maple syrup is one of New England's signature businesses, and the sugar maple trees are already feeling the effects of global warming. Since the winters aren't consistently cold, the sap flows earlier, and sugar makers tap the trees too soon. When the weather turns cold again, the flow stops, shortening the season and reducing supply dramatically.

Part 3
Extinction Stinks

Connect the Dots

Since animals first roamed the Earth more than 400 million years ago, they have faced the possibility of extinction caused by natural changes in their environment. The species that survived did so by adapting to these changes, whether it was during an ice age or a warming period. As the Earth naturally cooled and heated over time, the sea fell and rose. This created land bridges for animals to walk and plants to spread across. As animals bumped into one another and plants invaded other plants' territories, some survived and some did not. This is a natural process and it has worked for the planet Earth for millions of years. Until today. **Right now, there are too many plants and animals becoming extinct in too short a time.** Scientists predict that in just 50 years, more than one million species will be doomed to extinction because of global warming.

Species of frogs, butterflies, penguins, and polar bears are all threatened because they cannot adapt fast enough to the changes caused by increased greenhouse gases. Whether it's a disturbed forest ecosystem or shrinking sheets of ice to stand on, animals' ability to fulfill their primary needs for survival are disappearing.

Try to connect the dots of the plant and animal extinction hot spots — it's not a pretty picture.

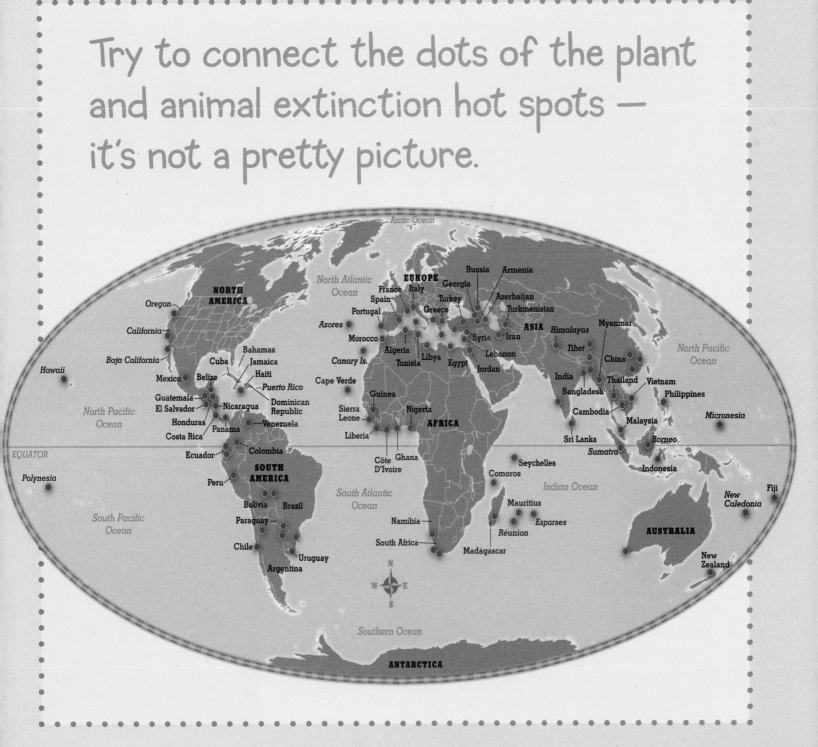

Walrus, Penguins, and Polar Bears, Oh, My!

Arctic Food Web

polar bears

↓

seals

↓

baleen whales · fish · walrus

↓

krill · clams · shellfish

↓

algae

↓

sunlight · ocean nutrients

They look like old men with long white mustaches. But as funny-looking as they are, walrus are at risk, too. They live life on the edge — the ice edge. The edge of the Arctic sea ice is an area rich with life. To get an idea of how rich, and how one animal or plant affects another, take a look at the food web.

Global warming is melting the sea ice, and the algae that normally live on the underside of the sea ice are disappearing because there is simply not enough area for them to breed in. Starting from the bottom of the food web, everything on it has something to eat. In other words, each downward arrow is a path to survival. A shortage of algae will affect everything above them in the food web, especially the walrus, which feed on clams and shellfish. **No food means no life. Extinction is next.**

Near Antarctica, on the frozen Weddell Sea, live the emperor penguins. These creatures, made famous from the movie *March of the Penguins,* make their nests on the frozen water. Sea ice needs to be thick enough to hold together for the duration of time it takes their eggs to hatch and their chicks to learn to live on their own. **As warmer temperatures and stronger winds thin out the Antarctic ice, the eggs and chicks are in danger of being stranded if the ice they're living on breaks off too soon and separates them from their mothers.** Some sea ice is also attached to land. Like an anchor on a ship, the land ice keeps the sea ice strong and sturdy. Unfortunately, we already know that the land ice is indeed melting. Eventually, these penguins may find their homes so threatened or damaged that they may not be marching anywhere.

Pretty soon, the zoo might be the only place to see a polar bear because scientists are predicting that those white fuzzy bears we all love will be extinct within 100 years. Polar sea ice is melting and breaking up more than it used to during summer months. Polar bears use the sea ice as a springboard into the ocean from which they hunt

That's a Lot of Clams

Walrus dive as deep as 250 feet (76.2 m) from the ocean's surface to forage snails, crabs, clams, and mussels. Adult walrus may scoop up as many as 3,000 to 6,000 clams at one feeding.

Left: A polar bear lies in the Arctic snow, after dying of starvation.

Wandering Bears

Hungry polar bears have been spotted in Halifax and Ontario, Canada, foraging for food in people's garbage cans. While it might seem like fun to have a polar bear in the city, it's exactly the opposite. It's dangerous for both humans and bears to come into contact with each other, especially when the bears are scared and confused, so far away from the sea ice that is their home.

ringed and bearded seals, their favorite dinner item. Seals also use ice as a platform from which to dive for food and on which they give birth to their pups. Without these platforms of ice, the seals are farther away and polar bears are forced to swim longer distances to find their prey. Sometimes on their journeys, the bears tire and drown. A drowning polar bear? Outrageous but true.

With fewer months of solid ice that the bears can use to dive from to look for food, their hunting season is shortened.

Scientists now estimate that because of the shrinking summer sea ice in the Arctic, we will lose two-thirds of our polar bears by the year 2050. Right now, there are 22,000 polar bears living on the Earth, but global warming will reduce that number to less than 7,500.

We would hate to imagine a world without our majestic polar bears.

It is the largest animal in the world, bigger than any dinosaur ever. Its magnificence has been recorded as far back as Jonah's adventures in the Bible. It is the great blue whale. And it happens to eat krill, one of the smallest sea creatures in the world. Krill, the blue whale's main food source, are shrimplike creatures smaller than the nail on your pinky finger. They are so small that one blue whale alone eats about 4 million krill every day. Through sound, blue whales communicate to one another about where they can find krill. When the whales arrive at a feeding spot, they use their baleen — bristles that hang from their upper jaw to their lower jaw — to take in great gulps of krill-filled ocean. Their powerful tongues then thrust the ocean water out, leaving only the krill to satisfy their enormous appetites. But because of global warming, these appetites are not being satisfied.

ON THE AIR

Penguins on the Radio

Radio transmitters are being strapped to the back of Adélie penguins in Antarctica. The idea is to see how far and how long this species of penguin goes to hunt for its food. Scientists discovered that some Adélies are traveling farther than ever before and are spending a longer time away from their rookeries, or nests. The reason? As in the case of the blue whales, thinner, less extensive sea ice is reducing the amount of krill, a food staple for the Adélie penguin. This forces them to work harder for the hunt. It also tires them out and shortens their life span.

Krill eat algae, and just as the walrus are finding their food sources diminishing, melting ice is making large portions of algae habitat disappear, especially in the Bering Sea and Hudson Bay areas of the lower Arctic. The krill simply aren't getting enough to eat, which, experts say, has brought down their population. In Antarctica, their number has decreased by a shocking 80 percent! Again, it's a food web problem. What happens to the little guys affects the big guys.

Don't Put Bleach in the Colors, Um, Corals!

I f you've ever gone snorkeling or seen a picture of coral reefs, then you know the rainbow of colors that is found in these magical places under the sea. Regrettably, the colors are being bleached out of the coral — much worse than making a mistake with the laundry.

Over the past 200 years, our oceans have absorbed about half of the CO_2 emissions that are in the atmosphere from the burning of fossil fuels. That's an enormous amount, which only shows how important the oceans are to our natural carbon cycle. But the oceans also absorb excess heat and solar radiation from the atmosphere. This is making the water warmer. And unfortunately, warmer oceans are putting coral at risk, big-time.

A Tiny Snail with a Big Bite

The coral reefs of Southeast Asia are home to the amazing cone snail. This tiny crawler produces a venom so powerful, it can paralyze a small fish in seconds. But it can also help ease the pain of a very sick person. Doctors have taken the cone snail's poison and turned it into a valuable medicine that has been helping many people. Who knows how many other medical miracles hiding in the coral reefs might never even be discovered if we destroy this precious ecosystem under the sea?

Coral enjoys a **symbiotic** relationship with a certain algae called zooxanthellae (don't try to pronounce it — we can't). Symbiotic means they both get something out of the deal. Kind of like you and your best friend: You've got a large, empty lot next door. He's got the foul ball from Game 2 of the World Series. Together, you can play one fantastic game of catch.

Coral reefs give algae a safe, sunny home, and algae provide food for coral. Zooxanthellae also give coral something else in this tidy arrangement: their brilliant colors. Coral aren't that pretty on their own; it's the zooxanthellae that have bright red, orange, and brown pigments.

Bleached coral off the coast of Halfway Island in the Keppel Island Group in 2002.

When water temperatures rise, the algae cannot photosynthesize — the chemical reaction that converts sunlight and CO_2 into sugars is blocked. This results in a buildup of chemicals that poison the zooxanthellae. Scientists are still trying to figure out this next part: In an act of survival, either the coral spits out the zooxanthellae or the toxic stuff that has built up in the zooxanthellae triggers something in the coral that hurts both of them. Either way, the coral loses its source of color and turns white, almost as if it has grown old overnight. **Bleached coral becomes weaker and more vulnerable to disease, predators, and storms — not to mention becoming a pretty feeble hideout for exotic fish.** Bleached coral *can* recover, but only if cooler water temperatures return.

As if bleaching weren't bad enough, coral has something else to stress about: acidity. All liquids are either acid or alkaline, which are chemical terms for the type of molecules that make up the liquids. The terms are opposites, meaning that if you mix an alkali with an acid, the alkali neutralizes it, or takes out the parts that make it so acidic. Orange juice is acidic. Toothpaste is alkaline. (This is why orange juice tastes so weird right after you brush your teeth!) Pure water is exactly in between, or neutral. Our oceans are alkaline. If the ocean chemistry falls closer to acid by even a small amount, it can affect everything. If only all this bleaching could just leave the coral squeaky clean, instead of fighting for their lives.

Fact: Increased CO_2 in our atmosphere is making the oceans more acidic. Coral (and all shellfish) need a certain level of calcium in order to make their hard shells. But higher acidity tilts the delicate balance of calcium in the water, reducing the amount available to coral and shellfish to build their protective skeletons. With some microscopic animals, it can even dissolve their shells.

61

Kiss This Toad Good-bye

There are many species of amphibians at risk of extinction from global warming. One-third of them, actually. This is quite a large number. If you have two best friends, it would be like one of you moving far away. The giant glass frog, the coqui tree frog, and the harlequin frog are just some of the amphibians at risk. But none was more spectacular than the golden toad. We say "was" because the last golden toad was seen on May 15, 1989.

Discovered in 1966, the golden toad was a small creature the color of a bright orange sunset. It was found in only one place — the Monteverde Cloud Forest Preserve in Costa Rica; in only one area — the upper slopes of the mountain. **Since the golden toad had such thin, sensitive skin, this cool, moist location was probably the only place where it could thrive.** There was something else that made the golden toad rare. For most of the year it lived underground in mossy burrows and came outside only for a few days to mate. You can imagine how exciting it was when researchers actually spotted one.

So what happened to these jewels of the forest? Let's look at the weather pattern of Monteverde. Monteverde is a cloud forest, which is different from a rain forest. Most of the year, the mountaintop is

The Monteverde Cloud Forest.

covered in a foggy mist, which keeps the area cool and comfortable for the thousands of animals and plants that live there. Scientists discovered that between 1976 and 1999 there were more and more days when the clouds didn't touch the mountaintop but instead floated just above it. This happened because the Pacific Ocean became warmer, heating up the air with evaporation, making it impossible for clouds to form as low as the mountaintop.

The warm air above Monteverde was forced to rise even higher to become cool enough to condense. **Without the lower mist, the forest dried up just enough to damage the golden toad's tender skin.**

We wish this were a fairy tale and that the handsome prince of the cloud forest, the golden toad, would reappear. But alas, this story is real. And no one knows how many more amphibians will suffer the same fate.

A Fungus Among Us

New research has found that the deadly chytrid fungus could have also been responsible for the golden toad's demise. This skin fungus thrives in areas where the nighttime temperature is warmer than average — exactly the conditions brought about by global warming in Central and South America.

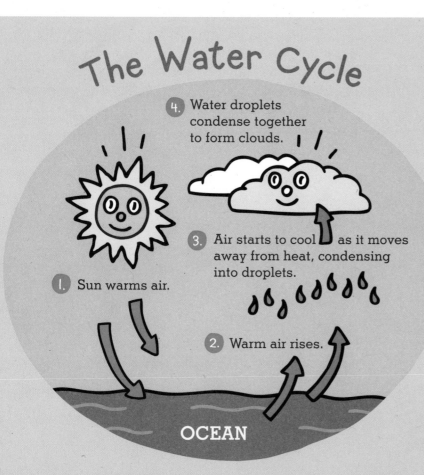

The Water Cycle

4. Water droplets condense together to form clouds.

3. Air starts to cool as it moves away from heat, condensing into droplets.

1. Sun warms air.

2. Warm air rises.

OCEAN

Up, Up, and Away

When the climate warms, plants and animals move toward the poles (north if they live in the northern half of the globe, south if they live in the southern half), seeking cooler temperatures much the same way you head to an air-conditioned mall or movie theater when the day gets too hot. But what happens to the plants and animals that already live near the poles? **Where do they go when there is nowhere else to run?**

Monarch butterfly.

64

Two types of butterflies are finding themselves in exactly this predicament. The Mountain Ringlet and Scotch Argus are northern butterflies that live in the mountain areas of Great Britain. While some butterfly species do thrive in warmer climates, these are mountain butterflies, meaning they need cool, moist mountain air to survive.

For three years, scientists trekked into the northern mountain areas of Scotland and England, visiting hundreds of locations where the mountain butterflies live. They looked under leaves and branches, flowers and rocks. They searched for butterflies, the plants their larvae (caterpillars) eat, and checked the overall condition of the area.

They discovered that certain butterflies were becoming extinct, yet it *appeared* to have nothing to do with global warming. At first. Some butterfly species had completely disappeared because their habitat was destroyed, either by farming or forestry encroaching on their space. But the Mountain Ringlet and the Scotch Argus had a perfectly fine habitat. All the luxuries a butterfly could ask for: plenty of food for caterpillars to eat, ample area in which to build cocoons, and not too many predators. It was a pretty nice setup.

So why did the scientists find so few of them? Climate change. **The butterflies that disappeared couldn't survive in the warmer temperatures and had no escape route.** Each stage of their life cycle — egg, larva, chrysalis, and adult — is dependent on the perfect temperature to make a successful transition to the next cycle. As temperatures warmed up at lower elevations, these butterflies simply died off.

Upper right: Scotch Argus butterfly.
Bottom left: Mountain Ringlet butterfly.

100, 99, 98 . . .

The red squirrel is literally being pushed off the mountain — Mount Graham, to be specific, 7,000 feet (2,134 m) above the desert of Arizona. The red squirrel's only habitat is called a sky island because it is an area isolated from other mountain forest regions. This means that plants and animals have been evolving there, untouched, since prehistoric times. But higher temperatures have changed this cool habitat, bringing insects that weaken and dry out trees, not to mention more deadly wildfires. All of which has brought the endangered Mount Graham red squirrel population down to about 100.

Some stronger butterflies in these species have managed to survive — the Scotch Argus by flying slightly farther north and the Mountain Ringlet by flying to higher altitudes — but their living space is quickly running out. Soon they will be as far north as they can possibly go, unless they want to fly to Iceland, Norway, or Sweden, distances far too great for their wings to carry them.

When butterflies fly away, we don't want them to go *away* away. Just far enough away so we can chase them across the lawn with nets or enjoy their beauty when they alight on a flower.

We now know that the way we are living is causing many species to become extinct. Is it okay for humans to interfere with nature so much? What is our responsibility to the polar bear, coral, frog, butterfly, and all the others? The time to act is now. Because we can still save many of the one million living creatures that are threatened with extinction! We have to work together to stop putting so much carbon dioxide into our air.

Give Me Shelter

Each winter, millions of monarch butterflies fly across the continent of North America to find shelter in the forests of Mexico. The forest acts like both an umbrella and a blanket, protecting the butterflies from too much rain, while maintaining the perfect climate — not too hot and not too cold — for them to survive. If the forests are clear-cut, then these lovely butterflies will have nowhere to hide.

Part 4
What You Can Do to Stop Global Warming

Clean Up Your Room!

I f you're like most kids, your room probably could use a little cleaning up. And if your mom's like most moms, she's probably been nagging you about it. She's right, by the way. You made the mess. You should clean it up. Well, the planet is kind of like one big messy bedroom. And guess what? The United States is making the biggest mess of all. We produce 25 percent of the world's carbon dioxide, making us the biggest polluter on the planet. So we need to play the largest part in helping to clean it up.

Mayors in cities all across America have signed an agreement to lower CO$_2$ emissions in their towns. The idea began in Seattle with Mayor Greg Nickels. It's called the U.S. Mayors Climate Protection Agreement, and its goal is to cut greenhouse gas emissions to levels below what they were in 1990 by 2012.

Here's what some cities have already done: Portland, Oregon, built 730 miles (1,175 km) of bike paths; Austin, Texas, gave tax breaks to homes and businesses for building green structures; Salt Lake City, Utah, converted 1,630 traffic signals to energy-efficient lightbulbs.

To find out if your mayor has already signed the agreement, check the Web site www.coolcities.us. If your city isn't listed there, then make a copy of the letter on page 73, stick it in an envelope, and send it to your mayor. If your city *is* there, do a victory dance, then find another city you've always liked and send the letter to its mayor. **The more mayors, the less CO$_2$!**

California, Here We Come!

Under the leadership of Governor Arnold Schwarzenegger, the state of California passed a landmark bill that made it the first state to limit global warming pollution. California has pledged to reduce carbon dioxide emissions to 1990 levels by the year 2020, and it also pledges to bring down levels to 80 percent below 1990 levels by the year 2050. We hope that other states across the nation will follow this example.

Cyclists take advantage of the new bike paths in Portland, Oregon.

To find out the name and address of a mayor, go to www.usmayors.org.

Dear Mayor _____,

Global warming is real and it's here to stay — unless we do something to stop it. There's an amazing agreement that more than 400 of your fellow mayors have signed. It's called the U.S. Mayors Climate Protection Agreement. It's a 12-step program that sets reasonable goals for your city to reduce carbon dioxide emissions to below what the levels were in 1990. Please join these other mayors in being leaders in the fight to stop global warming.

The kids of the world are depending on you.

Sincerely,

_____, Age_____

Or go paperless . . .

Check www.scholastic.com/downtoearthguide to download and e-mail this letter to your mayor!

How Many Concerned Kids Does It Take to Screw in a Lightbulb?

One. As long as it's a compact **fluorescent** bulb.

We think Thomas Edison would be thrilled to know that someone one-upped him by inventing a better lightbulb. It's not that his lightbulb wasn't incredible, it's just that all lightbulbs use electricity, which burns fossil fuels, which release greenhouse gases into the atmosphere and cause global warming. So why not try a bulb that uses *less* electricity and therefore releases *less* carbon dioxide?

A compact fluorescent lightbulb is 75% more energy-efficient than a regular lightbulb.

If you put a regular 60-watt **incandescent** bulb into a light you keep on most of the day, you might get 800 **lumens** for two months before it burns out. Lumens is a fancy-schmancy word for the total amount of light that a bulb is capable of generating.

With a 15-watt compact fluorescent bulb, you get 800 lumens for 20 months — ten times longer!

Compact fluorescent bulbs do the same amount of work as incandescents, yet use less energy, emit less CO_2, and last longer. It's like getting an upgrade on your iTunes software. Compact fluorescents are *new and improved* lightbulbs! If we sound like a commercial, we can't help it. This is an exciting and easy way to help stop global warming.

The reason compact fluorescent bulbs use less energy is they produce much less heat — which for a lightbulb is just wasted energy, because we only need the light. Touch a lit compact fluorescent bulb and it will feel cool.

Regular lightbulbs use four times more energy than compact fluorescent bulbs. Four times more is the equivalent of having four PlayStations instead of one. **What a waste.** You might even feel embarrassed by having so much. Similarly, we don't need all that wattage; we're using more than we need to do the job. The wasted electricity just burns more fossil fuels.

Though some compact fluorescent bulbs cost more than incandescent bulbs, you can end up saving at least 30 dollars on your family's electric bill over the life of the bulb.

Change a lightbulb today. All it takes is one person. And maybe a ladder.

A Bright Idea . . .

If every kid in America swapped one regular bulb for a compact fluorescent, we could prevent more than 30 *billion* pounds (13.6 billion kg) of greenhouse gas emissions and save enough energy to light more than 15 million homes for an entire year. It would be like taking 14 million cars off the road.

Gulp!

That's *plug* spelled backward, for all you word game experts. The reason why this page isn't called "plug" is because we want you to think about plugs differently and *un*plug your chargers. Believe it or not, leaving a charger plugged into the wall even after you remove your cell phone, iPod, GAME BOY, radio-controlled toy car, or MP3 player still drains energy. Plugged-in chargers use what's called phantom power, or standby power. In other words, it's power that you don't need and that is wasted. Just like Thomas Edison's hot lightbulb. Touch the plugged-in charger and it's warm.

Is Your Refrigerator *Running*?

The typical home contributes two times more global warming pollution than the average car. Because it is always running, the refrigerator is the single biggest energy-eating appliance in your house. To reduce your carbon footprint at home, urge your parents to buy appliances with a blue- or black-and-white ENERGY STAR sticker.

Saving or conserving what we don't need to use is one of the many solutions to global warming.

Actually, quite a large amount of home electricity is used up by phantom power. **Up to 10 percent of what your parents get billed for is stuff you turn off but don't unplug.** This includes not only chargers but televisions, computers, DVD players, even blow-dryers and electric toothbrushes.

The solution is simple. **Unplug those chargers from the wall. For all your appliances that you keep in one spot, like the computer and printer, or the TV, DVD player, and satellite or cable box, get a surge protector.** These are the long, funny-looking things with eight outlets for plugs that work like a normal power strip, only they're more efficient because they have an off switch that completely cuts off power from plugged-in appliances. **At the end of the day, turn off the surge protector.** It's just one switch and it can do a whole lot of good. Or *doog*.

Give It a Rest

Using the screen saver feature on your computer actually uses more energy than letting your computer go into sleep mode. Check the control panel or settings on your computer to make your computer automatically go into sleep mode after a few minutes. That screen saver with the 3-D shapes swirling around might be totally cool, but it's better to cool off planet Earth.

Paper or Plastic? Neither!

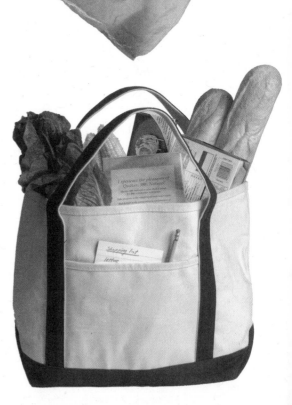

Next time you go to the grocery store with your parents or friends and the cashier asks you, "Paper or plastic?" say, "Neither!" Canvas bags are the way to go.

Frankly, it's hard to say which is worse, paper or plastic. Americans use 10 billion paper bags a year. Most brown bags are made of kraft paper, which is stronger than other paper. The only way to get paper that tough is to blend in virgin pulp — that is, pulp made from actual trees, not from recovered paper. Some of those trees come from old-growth forests that are more than 100 years old. **Think how much CO_2 is being released when those trees are cut down and how much they won't be able to capture in the future.** Not to mention the CO_2 pollution that goes into the air when the paper and pulp mills make all that paper.

Fact: To make 14 plastic bags, you'd need the same amount of petroleum that it would take to drive a car one mile (1.6 km).

Plastic bags are made from petroleum (that's oil, guys). Petroleum, taken out of the ground, is put through several chemical reactions until, finally, a puttylike material called a polymer is created. The polymer is the basis for all plastic. Although oil isn't being burned, it's certainly being wasted on the 100 billion bags that are thrown out each year.

Here is a perfect example of where we can conserve. **Oil is a nonrenewable resource. One day it will simply run out.** If everyone used reusable canvas bags, think of all the petroleum that would be saved. Of course, the real problem with plastic bags and other plastic products like water bottles comes from the manufacturing end. The plastic industry falls into the "industrial" category on the pie chart on page 7. A large part of that 29 percent of carbon dioxide emissions is their contribution.

Tote a canvas bag to the mall. For every store where you buy something, you save a plastic bag.

In terms of carrying your stuff around, canvas bags are a fantastic solution. No need to double-bag your heavy groceries with virgin fiber when you've got strong canvas supporting them. Ask your parents to keep a few in the car so you'll never have to choose between paper or plastic again.

An Emerald Green Solution

In Ireland, customers are charged money for paper or plastic bags. Almost no one takes them now!

Corny, but True

Americans buy more than 25 billion single water bottles a year, and, believe it or not, *2.5 million of them get thrown away every hour.* BIOTA, a water company in Colorado, makes its bottles out of corn. The bottles are completely biodegradable. That means that a BIOTA water bottle will decompose in 80 days. A regular plastic bottle takes more than 1,000 years to break down in a landfill! BIOTA also uses 30 to 50 percent less energy to make their bottles.

The Carbon (Re)Cycle

Hopefully, you already recycle. Maybe you separate your newspapers, bottles, and cans at home. Maybe you hand down your clothes to someone younger than you when you grow out of them. That's recycling, too. But in terms of global warming, paper recycling can make a difference. And just like making plastic bags, making paper uses a lot of energy. So the more we recycle paper or even do without it, the more energy we can save.

The more trees we cut down to make paper, the more CO_2 is released into the atmosphere and the fewer trees are left standing to absorb all the new CO_2 we've yet to produce.

Redwood trees of Muir Woods in northern California.

Here are some thoughts on reusing paper:

❧ That decaf mocha you or your parents like to take out from your favorite coffee place is probably served in a paper cup that used up a lot of energy to get from the tree into your hand. **Bringing in your own ceramic or travel mug with a lid saves the Earth 77.42 pounds (35.1 kg) of CO_2 over the entire life of the mug.**

❧ Your toilet paper, tissues, and paper towels are more than likely made from pulp that came from old-growth forests. Last year, one major paper products company used more than 2.7 million tons (2.5 million metric tons) of virgin timber to make its tissues, toilet paper, and paper towels, and destroyed hundreds of acres of Canada's ancient boreal forest in the process. Compare this with a company like Seventh Generation, which uses recycled fiber in nearly all of its pulp products. When you're at the store with your parents, check out the packages. **You want to buy paper goods that say they are made from 30 percent or more post-consumer waste.** (*Post-consumer waste* simply means stuff that has already been used.) Forty percent of the fiber in the world's toilet paper and tissues comes from trees never before touched by human hands. Should we be using ancient forests to wipe our noses?

❧ Your birthday cards are made from trees. **Fifteen trees are cut down and used to make one ton (907 kg) of the high-end glossy paper used in cards, magazines, and catalogs.** Another commonly used item, wrapping paper, is almost never made from recyclable material. Until there is recycled wrapping paper, you can use newspaper, discarded drawings and artwork, old magazines, even fabric remnants to wrap presents.

There are so many ways to recycle paper; these are just a few. Maybe you can come up with your own ideas and pass them on to someone else. That's what we call recycling!

Real Winners

Mountain Home High School, in Mountain Home, Arkansas, collected more than 6 million tons (5.4 million metric tons) of paper for recycling and received the 2006 School Recycling Award from the American Forest & Paper Association.

Think about what you use, how you use it, and where it goes when you're done.

Reading, Writing, and Saving Energy

We'd like to suggest that, in addition to all the things you're thinking about every day at school, like math tests and getting a good spot in line at the handball court, you think about another subject: saving energy.

Here are a few suggestions:

❀ **Start a no-idle rule in your school's car-pool lane.** Cars that sit for more than 30 seconds with their engines running use up more gasoline and emit more global warming pollution than if the motor is turned off and on again.

❀ **Suggest changing the paper in your school.** Talk to the folks in the main office and see if they use recycled paper. If they do, the packaging will say so. It should be made from at least 30 percent post-consumer waste. If not, ask them to make the change to help save trees that soak up carbon dioxide. If that doesn't work, circulate a school petition. Make sure your school makes photocopies on both sides of the paper!

❀ **Carpool with a friend.** Traveling together means there is one less car on the road, so you're cutting the car travel portion of your carbon footprint in half.

❀ **Reduce your school's carbon footprint by finding out the age of the school's water heater.** If it's older than five years, it's inefficient, which means too much CO_2 is being released when heating the water. Maybe there's enough money in the facilities budget to replace it.

❀ **Ask your principal about getting solar panels on the roof.** Across the country, elementary, middle, and high schools, as well as colleges, have installed solar panels to supplement or generate their own electricity. They are saving money and stopping global warming at the same time.

❀ **Start a no-waste policy in the cafeteria.** All food brought in must be in reusable containers. And all trash must go home with you. This helps kids and parents see how much is wasted at lunchtime. Five juice boxes in a week should give you a good idea. You should leave nothing but a warm bench where you sat for lunch.

❀ **Choose global warming as a topic for your next science, English, or social studies report.**

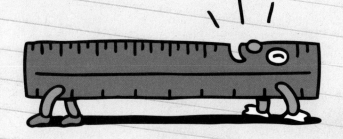

Campus Crusaders

Colleges are starting to do their part to stop global warming, too. The students of the University of Washington in Seattle agreed to raise their own fees so the school can start buying renewable electricity. At Texas A&M, they are using the cooking oil from the cafeteria to fuel the university's delivery trucks. The University of Miami offers a 50 percent parking discount for hybrid cars. And Cambridge University in England had a "Switch Off Day," reducing their electricity usage by around 5 percent just by taking simple steps like switching off unwanted lights and turning off computer monitors and printers. Imagine how much energy could be saved by doing this all year.

Once you've mastered this subject, you can even teach others about how to save energy!

🌿 **Conduct a recycling drive.** Bring what you collect to a local recycling center, where they might even pay you per pound!

🌿 **Put your money where your mouth is.** Take the money that your school makes on its next fund-raiser (whether it's selling chocolates or having a walkathon) and buy the school new compact fluorescent lightbulbs to replace their inefficient ones.

🌿 **Host an assembly on global warming.** Invite a speaker, pick up the DVDs *Too Hot Not to Handle* from HBO and *An Inconvenient Truth* (both produced by one of the authors of this book!), and have a discussion about global warming.

🌿 **Make global warming a community service project for your communion, confirmation, bar/bat mitzvah, or quinceañera.** You can donate a portion of your gift money or volunteer at an environmental organization.

Become Famous

(All You Need Is Energy)

Thirty fifth-grade students at Cherringon Elementary in Westerville, Ohio, created an energy club called the Wacky Watts. At Meece Middle School in Somerset, Kentucky, students took a field trip to a power plant, which inspired them to adopt a dock and clean up the water near their school. Other schools have received grant money to set up solar panels on campus. One group of students has even driven a hydrogen fuel cell car to other schools for demonstrations.

Why are all these kids famous? Because they were recognized at the National Youth Awards for Energy Achievement in Washington, D.C., and had their pictures taken with their representative in the U.S. Congress.

You and your school can become famous, too! All you have to do is submit your energy project to the National Energy Education Development — NEED, for short. **For more information about the NEED Awards program, please call (703) 257-1117 or go to www.need.org.**

Remember, knowledge is power: alternative energy power. Becoming famous is just a bonus.

The roof of Twenhofel Middle School in Independence, Kentucky, is lined with solar panels, which generate electricity.

Hybrid (hī-brəd)

n. Something of Mixed Origin or Composition

I f you cross a plum and an apricot, you get a pluot. Really. If you cross a soccer ball with a basketball, you get a socket. Not really. But if you cross a gasoline engine with a battery-powered motor, you *do* get a hybrid car.

A hybrid is high-tech, gets great gas mileage, earns your parents a tax break, and, best of all, it cuts greenhouse gas pollution. You fill up the tank at a regular gas station, only less often, and you don't have to plug it in. A hybrid car knows just when to use battery power and when to use engine power. It's also wonderfully peaceful at stop signs and red lights because the engine turns off when the car isn't moving.

How smart is that?

When this book went to press, there were hybrids on the road made by Honda, Lexus, Toyota, Ford, Mercury, Saturn, and Chevrolet. By 2008, drivers will be able to choose among 25 hybrid models. Just think how many there will be when you learn to drive! Next time you're on a road trip, play "count the hybrids." Your parents will start to notice them, too, and when they're ready for a new car, maybe they'll get their own hybrid.

We Love New York!

New York City has the largest fleet of hybrid buses in America. Now the city is converting its taxicabs into hybrids, too. Besides making passengers queasy from all that crazy driving, old NYC taxicabs get only 14 miles (22.5 km) to the gallon. A hybrid taxi can get 36 miles (58 km) to the gallon with one-third the greenhouse gas emissions!

86

The Alternatives Rock

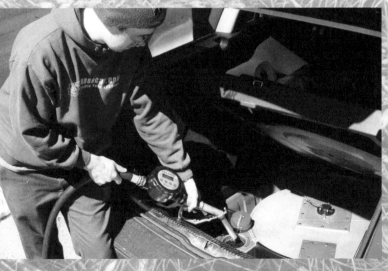

T he good news is that there are already great alternative fuels that provide clean substitutes for oil.

Ethanol

Ethanol is an alcohol-based fuel made from turning starch crops (like corn, barley, and wheat) into simple sugars. When combined with regular gasoline, it's called E85, which means 85 percent ethanol and 15 percent gasoline. Already widely used in Sweden and Brazil, ethanol can help reduce your car's greenhouse gas emissions, and nearly all 50 U.S. states have pump stations that now offer this type of alternative fuel.

Flex-fuel vehicles are cars that run on both gas and ethanol. It costs very little to turn a regular car into a flex-fuel vehicle, and there are about five million of them on the road in the United States today. Made by all the major carmakers, flex-fuel vehicles definitely use less gas, but the best of both worlds is the hybrid flex-fuel car. Ford, for example, is making one now.

Filling up a grease car, which runs solely on vegetable oil.

Fact: One less barrel of imported oil is needed for every 28.3 gallons (107 l) of ethanol used.

Biodiesel

Biodiesel, another alternative fuel, is made from a mixture of vegetable oil and alcohol, and can power any diesel engine. Some people have gone a step further and converted their modern diesels to run only on vegetable oil. The only side effect we've heard about is an unusual craving for French fries.

Speedy Clean

The Indy 500 is now using 100 percent fuel-grade ethanol to power its cars. An engine running on ethanol performs better than one that runs on regular gasoline, and track records have already been broken. And because this type of ethanol packs more energy per gallon than traditional race car fuel, these race cars can go faster and farther.

Since biodiesel is made from crops grown by farmers in the United States, it can help us become less dependent on fuels imported from other countries.

We've Got the Power

We've spent a lot of time talking about why burning fossil fuels is so bad. Now it's time to hear about why the future of fuel is good. There are other ways we can get our electricity, drive our cars, and manufacture our products. It's called renewable energy, meaning energy that won't run out and that pollutes less. Much less. It can also renew the wallet, so to speak, because governments and corporations around the world that have chosen renewable energy have seen their economies grow by creating new jobs and saving on energy costs. Here are some examples.

All together, wind machines in the United States can produce enough electricity to power a city the size of Chicago.

Wind Power

From the time of the ancient Phoenicians, the world's first sailors, people have known how to use the wind for power. The Dutch were the first to harness wind power on land, using windmills to pump water from the Rhine River in the 1600s. Today, a typical wind turbine — or a really big windmill — can generate enough power to run electricity in more than 1,000 homes.

89

A Stinky Solution

When animals eat hay and grain, the carbohydrate energy stored in the plant food can be found in their poop. One farm in Wisconsin actually uses cow dung to make electricity. As the cow waste breaks down, it releases methane gas. A manure digester machine speeds up this process and captures the methane. The gas is then used to fuel a small power plant. This process also prevents the methane from escaping into the atmosphere, where it would become a heat-trapping greenhouse gas!

Some people are helping to stop global warming by using the green power option on their electric bill. By paying a small amount (about $3 if your bill is $50 a month) to run wind turbines, the electric company doesn't need to burn as much coal. If more homes and businesses use the green power option, the price of wind power will go down even more!

Solar Power

Though the sun is about 93 million miles (150 million km) away from Earth, it can power anything from pool heaters to cars as long as it is harnessed properly. Solar panels (also called photovoltaic cells), solar hot water systems, and solar-thermal (thermal = heat) power stations are three ways to use the sun's energy. They work by collecting the sun's heat and transferring that energy through pipes to your home or directly to the grid that supplies power to a whole city. Some solar power systems also store energy so you have reserve power even when the sun goes down.

The 2006 Dell-Winston School Solar Car Challenge, with cars powered by nothing but the sun.

Geothermal Power

The word *geothermal* literally means "Earth heat." If you traveled 10,000 feet (3,048 m) belowground, the temperature of the rock would be hot enough to boil water. (If water deep down in the Earth gets heated by this rock and comes up through a crack in the Earth's surface, this phenomenon is called a hot spring or a geyser.) In Iceland, many buildings and swimming pools are heated with geothermal hot water. **Even power plants can run on geothermal power.** Holes are drilled into the ground and pipes are lowered into the steam or hot water, like an eyedropper is inserted into eyedrops. The hot water feeds into a turbine with spinning blades. The shaft from the turbine is connected to a generator to make electricity. If you've ever seen a geothermal power plant, that isn't smoke coming out of it, but steam being released in the cooling process. **Geothermal energy isn't used much right now, but research is under way to learn how to get heat from the deep, dry rocks inside the Earth's crust and, possibly, even deeper, from the Earth's magma.**

Old Faithful Geyser, in Yellowstone National Park.

91

Hydropower

If you've ever been tossed and turned about by an ocean wave, then you understand the power of water. Hydropower uses moving water, either from rivers or dams, to create energy. A hydroelectric dam works by holding back water behind a wall. The water is released through a pipe and pushed against blades in a turbine, causing them to turn. The turbine then spins a generator and makes electricity, which travels over long distances to your home, school, and favorite corner store.

The Grand Coulee Dam is located on the Columbia River in Washington State.

Fact: 20% of the world's electricity comes from waterpower.

Biomass Power

Believe it or not, dead trees, yard clippings, wood chips, straw, underbrush, switch grass, and composting material can produce electricity, heat, and fuel. Before this stuff was trash, it was alive, which means it was part of the **carbon cycle**. And that means it stored energy in the form of carbon. When the plants were alive, the photosynthesis process took the sun's energy and converted it to carbohydrates. That energy is recaptured when biomass is burned in huge boilers. The heat released from this process is used to turn water into steam, which turns a steam turbine to create electricity. Recent discoveries have even found a way to convert leaves and plant stalks into the alternative fuel ethanol.

If we used just one-eighth of what the world produces in biomass each year, it would provide all the energy needs of every single person on the planet.

There is no single solution. In fact, we need *every* solution. The future holds even more solutions, and you'll be a part of that.

What Do You Want to Be When You Grow Up?

A Sustainable Career

If something is sustainable, it will last and never be depleted. Your love for your pet is sustainable, even though your cat might pee on your bedspread or your dog might chew your favorite flip-flops. Bamboo, a quick-growing grass that is planted just for the purpose of constructing furniture and floors, is sustainable. Wind and solar power are sustainable.

It's never too early to dream about what you want to be when you grow up. Here are a few careers that you might want to think about:

Forest Resource Officer

Promotes respect for the web of life in a forest ecosystem. Takes action to protect the biodiversity of forests and selects species for reforestation. Can work in national parks, universities, or recycled-paper mills.

Glacial Geologist

Focuses on the Earth's past and present as it relates to the physical properties and movement of glaciers and ice sheets. Discovers how glaciers were formed and what has happened to them since their formation. Can work as a university professor or in an engineering firm.

Hydrologist

Studies the physical properties of underground and surface water. Examines rain — its rate of infiltration into the soil, its movement through the Earth, and its return to the ocean and atmosphere. Studies flood control and groundwater contamination issues. Can work as an environmental consultant in an architectural firm or for the Department of Defense.

Environmental Communicator

Gathers support to protect threatened ecosystems. Informs people about crucial environmental issues through newspaper or magazine stories, Web sites, videos, films, and photographs that show sustainable living and showcase nature. Can work for the government, in radio or television, or at museums.

Agricultural Technologist

Helps farmers with planning, cultivating, harvesting, and storing crops. Demonstrates environmentally sustainable farming techniques and suggests what crops to grow in particular soils and growing conditions. Can work in a small village or a big city.

Wind Development Associate

Helps with the construction of wind farms. Analyzes wind, sites, and environmental data. Can work at either a wind farm or a corporate office.

A career in the environmental field is sustainable because, in the future, we will need more and more experts who understand global warming.

Biofuels Engineer

Produces renewable fuels such as biodiesel, biomass, ethanol, and biogas. Can work at a biofuel plant and travel to farms where seed crops are grown.

Solar Sales Representative

Designs solar power systems for homes or businesses and convinces people to switch to solar power. Can work for a solar energy firm but can also do some work from home.

Atmospheric Scientist, or Meteorologist

Predicts the weather. Identifies climate trends by studying past and present weather. Studies air pressure, temperature, humidity, and wind speed. Can work for the government at weather stations or in broadcasting.

There are so many wonderful careers in the environmental field that it would have taken 20 more pages to list them all. We didn't think we could "sustain" your interest for that long.

Live for Today, but Protect the Future

Former Norwegian prime minister Gro Harlem Brundtland is credited with introducing the groundbreaking concept of "sustainable development" onto the world stage. The idea is that everyone — businesspeople, politicians, farmers, doctors, lawyers, environmentalists, parents, and schoolchildren, too — is responsible for creating a healthy and happy world today that will ensure the ability of future generations to meet their own needs for a healthy and happy tomorrow.

What Else You Can Do

Let Your Fingers Do the Marching

In August 1963, when Martin Luther King, Jr., led the March on Washington, 250,000 people marched along with him in support of civil rights for blacks and minorities. It was the largest demonstration ever held in the U.S. capital. In April 1970, millions turned up in cities all over the United States for the first celebration of Earth Day. In fact, the Earth Day events led to the passage of two landmark laws, the Clean Air Act and the Endangered Species Act, as well as the formation of the Environmental Protection Agency (EPA).

The thing about marches is that they generally last only one day. But now there's a way to march to stop global warming every day. It's called a virtual march and it's as easy to do as browsing and clicking. **The idea is to get as many people as possible to use the Internet instead of the pavement to register their concern for the environment. The message you'll be telling our leaders is that we want solutions to global warming. Now.**

Go to www.stopglobalwarming.org. When you see some of the other folks who are marching virtually, you'll know what good company you're in.

C. C. + S.

It's not someone's initials on the bathroom wall. It stands for Carbon Capture and Storage, and the name says it all. This is a way to prevent carbon dioxide emissions from getting into our atmosphere in the first place. Here are just two areas in which energy companies are currently doing research:

1. Capturing CO_2 from the smokestacks of power plants and feeding it to a hothouse of hungry algae.

2. Burying CO_2 deep in the ground by pumping it from the power plant directly into old oil and natural gas fields.

Carbon Capture and Storage is an exciting solution. And it lasts a lot longer than a school crush.

Go Carbon Neutral

The band Coldplay went a step further than marching. They made their carbon footprint disappear. Making an album uses up a lot of energy, from running the recording studio to producing all of those CD jewel boxes to driving the trucks and planes that have to get them to the stores. After they cut their CD *A Rush of Blood to the Head*, Coldplay bought 10,000 mango trees for villagers in Karnataka, India. The idea is that the trees will provide a carbon sink for all the CO_2 the band emitted in making and selling its CD. Of course, we can't plant enough trees to absorb all the CO_2 released from the amount of fossil fuels we are burning now, but it's one of the many things we can do.

There are many companies that can help a rock band — or a family — go carbon neutral. Here are two of them: www.carbonfund.org and www.nativeenergy.com.

Come Up with the Next Great Idea

You never know who or where a solution will come from. A ski resort in Andermatt, Switzerland, figured that since their glacier was melting, they'd protect it from heat, solar energy, and rain. They covered the whole glacier, an area more than 32,300 square feet (3,000 m²) wide, with insulating foam — kind of like putting the glacier in a giant thermos. It cost a bundle, but the insulation can be reused after every ski season.

A company called Simple Shoes recycles car tires and plastic milk jugs to make shoes for both kids and adults, saving the energy it would take if they made shoes from new rubber and plastic. Their shoes also contain materials from other renewable sources like cork trees and jute bushes, which don't require the cutting of old-growth trees to get at the stuff inside. The flip-flops even make tire-tread marks when you walk on the beach!

Kenny Luna, an eighth-grade teacher in New York, challenged everyone in his school and the surrounding community to change one lightbulb to a compact fluorescent bulb and even got Home Depot to donate the bulbs.

Anne Lasker, an elementary school parent in Los Angeles, started a Trashion Show, where kids make their outfits out of recycled material.

And an eighth-grade boy in California made a CD of original songs that he wrote and recorded at home on his computer. He then sold the CDs at school and donated the money to a stop global warming cause.

Become a Global Warming Activist

We hope you will become a global warming activist. If you can change the way you think, you can help others change the way they think. If you can make one small change in your actions, like unplugging a charger from the wall, then you'll set an example for others to do it, too. **We need big, bold ideas for this global problem.** So let's all get down to Earth and start thinking. No idea is too outrageous. No solution is too far from possibility. Will you be the one to come up with a new solution?

The Earth is depending on you!

Words To Know

albedo effect
The amount of light a body or surface reflects and the amount of light that is absorbed.

carbon cycle
The process in the ecosystem by which carbon is exchanged among organisms, oceans, atmosphere, and land.

carbon footprint
A measure of the amount of carbon dioxide a business or individual emits through the burning of fossil fuels.

carbon sink
An area of the Earth that permanently removes carbon dioxide from the atmosphere and binds it in organic compounds. The most important carbon sinks are the world's oceans and forests.

circumpolar
Wind, ocean currents, stars, animals, people — anything that moves around either pole of the Earth.

clear-cutting
The cutting or harvesting of all of the trees in an area at one time with no plan for regenerating or renewing the forest.

equilibrium
A state of balance kept between opposing forces or elements so that no change occurs.

fluorescent
A lamp in which a phosphor coating transforms ultraviolet energy into visible light. Uses far less electrical energy than an incandescent lamp.

fossil fuel
The remains of prehistoric plant and animal life, such as coal, oil, and natural gas, that are used to provide energy when burned.

global warming
An increase in the Earth's average temperature that causes changes in climate patterns worldwide.

green
Also known as "going green"; the adoption of a sustainable lifestyle that respects the environment while actively working to curb our carbon footprint and leave the world better than we found it.

greenhouse gas
A heat-trapping gas in the Earth's atmosphere that is also released from the burning of fossil fuels.

incandescent
A common form of artificial light in which a filament contained in a vacuum is heated to brightness by an electric current. Only 5 percent of the energy output of incandescent lighting is light, while the remaining 95 percent is heat.

long-wave energy
Energy that leaves the Earth by being radiated from the surface back into the atmosphere.

lumen
A unit of measurement quantifying the amount of light emitted from a light source.

organism
Any individual living creature, made of either one cell or multiple cells.

permafrost
A layer of soil below the Earth's surface where the temperature has remained below freezing for two or more years.

polar ice cap
The permanent mass of sea ice that forms a jagged circle around the North Pole, and that covers about 70 percent of the Arctic Ocean.

sediment
A material, deposited by wind, water, or glaciers, that sinks to the bottom of a body of water.

short-wave energy
The light energy that comes directly from the sun.

stratification
The physical layering of ocean water resulting from density differences caused by salt or temperature variations.

symbiotic
A close and prolonged relationship between two or more different kinds of organisms in which both benefit.

water vapor
The water present in the atmosphere in a gaseous form.

Suggestions for Further Reading

Braasch, Gary. *Earth under Fire: How Global Warming Is Changing the World.* Berkeley, Ca.: University of California Press, 2007.

Gore, Al. *An Inconvenient Truth: The Crisis of Global Warming.* New York: Viking Children's Books, 2007.

Langley, Andrew. *Hurricanes, Tsunamis and Other Natural Disasters.* Boston: Kingfisher, 2006.

Revkin, Andrew. *The North Pole Was Here: Puzzles & Perils at the Top of the World.* Boston: Kingfisher, 2006.

Sussman, Art, Ph.D. *Dr. Art's Guide to Planet Earth.* White River Junction, Vt.: Chelsea Green, 2000.

———. *Dr. Art's Guide to Science.* Hoboken, N.J.: Jossey Bass, 2006.

Taylor, Barbara. *How to Save the Planet.* New York: Franklin Watts, 2000.

Vogel, Carole Garbuny. *Human Impact (The Restless Sea).* New York: Franklin Watts, 2003.

Cool Web Sites to Check Out

adventureecology.com
Here's an interactive game that lets you travel the world as an eco-adventurer to find global warming hot spots.

planetfriendly.com
This Web site certifies products, places, and processes that help the planet instead of harming it. One of the things you'll discover is plates, cups, straws, and other food containers made from corn. Look for them at the food court in your mall and at supermarket salad bars.

stopglobalwarming.org

You can sign up here for the virtual march and also order the coolest accessories around: leather bracelets that say STOP GLOBAL WARMING and flip-flops that have the Stop Global Warming logo on the straps.

stopglobalwarming.msn.com
On this MSN Web site, you can get up-to-the-minute global warming news and energy saving tips, and watch videos or read interviews of your favorite athletes, musicians, and actors talking about global warming. Windows Live Spaces will also help you create your own blog about global warming.

nrdc.org
This is the official Web site for the Natural Resources Defense Council, one of the world's best watchdogs for our environment. Click on "Kids Make Waves" to learn all about the many ways you can help.

scholastic.com/ downtoearthguide
This Web site will provide even more down-to-Earth facts and background information on this book, including downloadables, e-cards, and more.

Source Notes

Authors' Note

Page x *The third installment of IPCC's four-part report* . . . : IPCC, 2007: Climate Change 2007: The Physical Science Basis. Contribution of Working Group I to the Fourth Assessment Report of the Intergovernmental Panel on Climate Change [Solomon, S., D. Qin, M. Manning, Z. Chen, M. Marquis, K. B. Avery, M. Tignor and H. L. Miller (eds.)]. Cambridge University Press, Cambridge, United Kingdom and New York, NY, USA.

Page x *the Stern Report, issued in England* . . . : Stern, N., et al. *The Economics of Climate Change: The Stern Review.* HM Treasury: London, 2006. Accessed online May 9, 2007, at http://www.hm-treasury.gov.uk/independent_reviews/stern_review_economics_climate_change/sternreview_index.cfm.

Page x *Scientists at the National* . . . : Stroeve, J., et al. "Arctic sea ice decline: Faster than forecast." *Geophysical Research Letters,* Vol. 34, L09501, doi:10.1029/2007GL029703 (2007).

Page x *"Noah's Ark"* . . . : Poggioli, Sylvia. "Climate Change Threatens European Landmarks." *NPR Morning Edition* 17 August 2007.

Page x *China is expected* . . . : Bradsher, Keith. "China to Pass U.S. in 2009 in Emissions." *The New York Times* 7 November 2006; Collier, Robert. "A Warming World: China about to pass U.S. as world's top generator of greenhouse gases." *San Francisco Chronicle* 5 March 2007.

Page xi *Australia and Canada* . . . : "Canada to ban incandescent lightbulbs by 2012." *Reuters* 25 April 2007.

Page xi *The city of San Francisco* . . . : Goodyear, Charlie. "S.F. First City to Ban Plastic Shopping Bags." *San Francisco Chronicle* 28 March 2007.

Page xi *including Home Depot* . . . : *Sierra Magazine* May/June 2007, p. 33.

Page xi *like Boston's Fenway Park* . . . : Van Voorhis, Scott. "Wally Would Be Proud as Fenway Park Goes Green." *Boston Herald* 21 September 2007.

Page xi *Former Vice President Al Gore* . . . : www.nobelprize.org.

Page xi *The U.S. government is working* . . . : Fialka, John J., and Kathryn Kranhold. "Lights Out for Old Bulbs?" *The Wall Street Journal* 13 September 2007.

Part One: It's Getting Hot in Here

Page 2 *Carbon dioxide is released* . . . : E-mail correspondence with Dr. Susan Hassol, climate analyst and author.

Page 3 *Cars, factories, and electric power plants* . . . : www.fueleconomy.com.

Page 3 *global warming is causing* . . . : Tebaldi, Claudia, et al. "Going to the Extremes: An Intercomparison of Model-Simulated Historical and Future Changes in Extreme Events." *Climatic Change* 79.3/4 (2006): 185–211.

Page 3 *Global warming is also causing less snow* . . . : Stauth, David. "Global Warming Poses Risk to Pacific Northwest Snowpack, Ski Resorts." *Oregon State University News and Communications Services* 7 March 2006.

Page 4 *Both glass-covered greenhouses* . . . : Interview with John Steelman, Campaign Director, Natural Resources Defense Council Climate Center.

Page 7 *Maybe an earthquake* . . . : Interview with John Steelman, Campaign Director, Natural Resources Defense Council Climate Center.

Page 7 *Where does all this CO_2 Come From?*: CO_2 emissions by end-use sector, Energy Information Administration, 2004; Emissions of greenhouse gases in the US 2004, Report #DOE/EIA-0573(2004); US Emissions Inventory 2006, Environmental Protection Agency, ESEPA #430-R-06-002.

Page 13 *Keeling Curve graph*: Flannery, Tim. *The Weather Makers.* New York: Atlantic Monthly Press, 2005, p. 25.

Page 15 *One tree can absorb the amount of CO_2* . . . : Shropshire, David E. *Global Climate Change.* Idaho National Engineering & Environmental Laboratory, July 2002.

Page 16 *Inside the Dome C ice core* . . . : E-mail correspondence with Eric Wolff, British Antarctic Survey.

Page 16 *The amount of CO_2 in our atmosphere today is at 27 percent higher* . . . : E-mail correspondence with Dr. Susan Hassol, climate analyst and author.

Page 18 *You can see this relationship for yourself* . . . : Siegenthaler, Urs, et al. "Stable Carbon Cycle-Climate Relationship During the Late Pleistocene." *Science* 310 (2005): 1313–1317.

Page 18 *Well, the Earth's average temperature* . . . : EPA Climate Change, Basic Information. http://epa.gov/climatechange/basicinfo.html.

Page 19 *Eleven out of twelve of the years* . . . : IPCC AR4 WG1 Summary for Policymakers, p. 5.

Page 19 *July 2005 to June 2006* . . . : National Climatic Data Center (NCDC). www.ncdc.noaa.gov/oa/climate/research/2006/jul/jul06.html.

Page 20 *Well, one degree hotter for the world on average* . . . : IPCC AR4 WG1, p. 5.

Page 20 *Warm, westerly winds* . . . : E-mail correspondence with Dr. Gareth Marshall, climatologist for the British Antarctic Survey.

Page 22 *Something that is not a source* . . . : Interview with John Steelman, Campaign Director, Natural Resources Defense Council Climate Center.

Page 22 *Over forty years, one acre* . . . : Shropshire, David E. *Global Climate Change.* Idaho National Engineering & Environmental Laboratory, July 2002.

Page 22 *6.6 billion*: World Population Clock, http://www.census.gov/main/www/popclock.html.

Page 22 *Every two seconds* . . . : Greenpeace. "The Amazon's Major Threat: Illegal logging." Press report July 2000.

Page 23 *the fire season has become two months longer:* Westerling, A. L. "Warming and Earlier Spring Increase Western U.S. Forest Wildfire Activity." *Science* 313 (2006): 940–943.

Page 23 *Forests and soils store carbon dioxide* . . . : Conversation with Nigel Pervis, The Nature Conservancy.

Page 24 *The problem now is that with so much CO$_2$* . . . : Correspondence with Daniel A. Lashof, Ph.D., Science Director, Natural Resources Defense Council Climate Center.

Page 24 *It has to do not only* . . . : Interview with Joel Reynolds, Director, Natural Resources Defense Council Marine Mammal Protection Program.

Page 25 *If CO$_2$ emissions continue to rise* . . . : Correspondence with Dr. Susan Hassol, climate analyst and author.

Page 26 *The average American adult* . . . : IPCC AR4 WGI, SPM, p. 3.

Page 26 *It's an amount that scientists* . . . : Interview with Tim Greeff, Campaign Director, Natural Resources Defense Council Climate Center.

Page 27 *Using a screensaver* . . . : Correspondence with Noah Horowitz, Senior Scientist, Natural Resources Defense Council; http://www.energystar.gov/index.cfm?c=energy_awareness.bus_energy_use for conversions.

Page 27 *Turning on the lights* . . . : Energy Information Agency, Department of Energy, www.eia.doe.gov.

Page 27 *Taking a bath* . . . : The number is based on a flow rate of 5 gallons per minute into a tub filling in 4 minutes and heating 20 gallons of water, then converting Btu to therms to kWh to pounds of CO$_2$. Ibid; www.showerheadsrus.com/sp-bin/spirit?page=24&CATALOG=5.

Page 27 *Riding in a car* . . . *(based on driving to school 2.5 miles each way)*: The median distance to school for children ages 5–15 years, http:/www.cdc.gov/mmwr/preview/mmwrhtml/mm5132al.htm.

Page 27 *. . . in a car that gets 20 miles per gallon*: Conversation with Tim Greeff, Campaign Director, Natural Resources Defense Council Climate Center, for conversions of mpg to lbs of CO$_2$.

Page 27 *Now, if you take* . . . : U.S. Census Bureau, 2000 Census.

Page 27 *Because CO$_2$ stays in the atmosphere* . . . : IPCC AR4 WGI, p. 11, "Scientific Assessment of Ozone Depletion," 10.21.

Part Two: Weird, Wacky Weather

Page 35 *But overall, rainfall is increasing* . . . : Climate Change 2001, Figure 15. Robert T. Watson, Chair, Intergovernmental Panel on Climate Change, at the resumed Sixth Conference of parties to the United Nations Framework Convention on Climate Change. 19 July 2001.

Page 37 *as the temperature gets cooler* . . . : Interview with John Steelman, Campaign Director, Natural Resources Defense Council Climate Center.

Page 37 *While it is true* . . . : E-mail correspondence with Dr. Heidi Cullen, The Weather Channel climate expert and host of *The Climate Code*.

Page 37 *In the year 2000* . . . : "Natural disasters at record level in 2000." *Reuters* 29 December 2000.

Page 37 *Even in Asia* . . . : International Monetary Fund. "Picture This: Hit by Disaster." *Finance & Development* 40.3 (2003).

Page 37 *The pools of standing water* . . . : www.westnile.ca.gov/mosquito_control.html.

Page 38 *But with warmer temperatures caused by global warming* . . . : Correspondence with Dr. Susan Hassol, climate analyst and author.

Page 39 *Here are the areas* . . . : NCDC. www.ncdc.noaa.gov/oa/climate/research/2006/jul/us-drought.html.

Page 43 *And 2007 is expected* . . . : www.abcnews.go.com/us/Globalwarming/wirestory?id=2769263.

Page 44 *Already in the last 100 years* . . . : IPCC TAR WG1 SPM, p. 4.

Page 44 *Half of it* . . . : EPA, Climate Change Science, "Sea Level Changes," http://www.epa.gov/climatechange/science/recentslc.html.

Page 44 *climatologists are most worried about the Greenland ice sheet*: "L.A. Times Special Report: Greenland's Ice Sheet is Slip-Sliding Away." *Los Angeles Times* 25 June 2006.

Page 45 *If the Greenland ice sheet melts completely* . . . : "L.A. Times Special Report: Greenland's Ice Sheet is Slip-Sliding Away." *Los Angeles Times* 25 June 2006; IPCC AR4.

Page 46 *But scientists are predicting that within 25 years* . . . : Yohe, Evelyne. "Sizing up the Earth's Glaciers." NASA Earth Science Enterprise Data and Services, National Snow and Ice Data Center DAAC, 22 June 2004.

Page 48 *Poison Ivy* . . . : Mohan, Jacqueline E., et al. "Biomass and Toxicity Responses of Poison Ivy to Elevated Atmospheric CO$_2$." *PNAS* 103.24 (2006): 9086–9089.

Page 48 *Fall leaves* . . . : New England Regional Assessment Group. *Preparing for a Changing Climate: The Potential Consequences of Climate Variability and Change*. New England Regional Overview, U.S. Global Change Research Program. University of New Hampshire, 2001.

Page 48 *Ski seasons get shorter*: Hecox, Walter E., et al, eds. *The 2005 Colorado College State of the Rockies Report Card*. Colorado Springs, Colorado: The Colorado College State of the Rockies Project, 2005.

Page 49 *Allergies are triggered and asthma worsens*: Ziska, L. H., et al. "Cities as harbingers of climate change: common ragweed, urbanization and public health." *Journal of Allergy Clinical Immunology* 111.2 (2003): 290–295.

Page 49 *Outdoor ice rinks shrink*: Correspondence with Eric Chivian, M.D., Director, Center for Health and the Global Environment, Harvard Medical School.

Page 49 *Disease-carrying ticks and mosquitoes* . . . : Patz, Jonathan, et al. "Impact of Regional Climate Change on Human Health." *Nature* 438.7066 (2005): 310–317.

Page 49 *ticks and mosquitoes can now exist* . . . : E. Lindgren, L. Tälleklint, and T. Polfeldt. "Impact of climatic change on the northern latitude limit and population density of the disease-transmitting European Tick, *Ixodes ricinus*." *Environmental Health Perspectives* 108.2 (2000): 119–23.

Page 49 *Bark beetle population explodes*: Juday, Glenn. "Chapter 14: Forests, land management and agriculture" in *Arctic Climate Impact Assessment, Scientific Report*. New York: Cambridge University Press, 2005.

Page 49 *Pancakes get drier*: Correspondence with Eric Chivian, M.D., Director, Center for Health and the Global Environment, Harvard Medical School.

Part Three: Extinction Stinks

Page 52 *Scientists predict that in just 50 years* . . . : "China Gets Dutch Help to Fight Floods, Droughts." *Reuters* 11 April 2007, http://www.planetark.com/avantgo/dailynewsstory.cfm?newsid=41333; "UN warns world on Africa drought." *BBC News* 23 February 2006, http://news.bbc.co.uk/2/hi/africa/4744812.stm; Marks, Kathy. "Australia's epic drought: The situation is grim." *The Independent, UK* April 2007; U.S. Drought Monitor, as of April 2007, http://www.drought.unl.edu/dm/monitor.html.

Page 57 *Scientists now estimate* . . . : Durner, George M., et al. "Predicting the Future Distribution of Polar Bear Habitat in the Polar Basin." U.S. Department of the Interior. United States Geological Survey.

Page 57 *And it happens to eat* . . . : Interview with Joel Reynolds, Director, Natural Resources Defense Council Marine Mammal Protection Program.

Page 59 *Over the past 200 years or so* . . . : "Ocean Acidification Due to Increasing Atmospheric Carbon Dioxide." *The Royal Society* 30 June 2005.

Page 61 *Bleached coral can recover* . . . : E-mail correspondence with Dr. Susan Hassol, climate analyst and author.

Page 61 *Coral (and all shellfish)* . . . : E-mail correspondence with Dr. Susan Hassol, climate analyst and author.

Page 62 *One-third of them, actually*: Pounds, Alan, et al. "Widespread Amphibian Extinctions from Epidemic Disease Driven by Global Warming." *Nature* 439.7073 (2006): 161–167; Thomas, Chris D., et al. "Extinction Risk from Climate Change." *Nature* 427.6970 (2004): 145–147.

Page 62 *For most of the year* . . . : Flannery, Tim. *The Weather Makers*. New York: Atlantic Monthly Press, 2005, pp.115–19.

Page 63 *Scientists discovered that* . . . : Flannery, Tim. *The Weather Makers*. New York: Atlantic Monthly Press, 2005, pp.115–19.

Page 63 *New research has found that the deadly chytrid fungus* . . . : Pounds, A. & Savage, J. 2004. *Bufo periglenes*. In: IUCN 2006. *2006 IUCN Red List of Threatened Species*. www.iucnredlist.org.

Page 64 *When the climate warms, plants and animals move* . . . : Correspondence with Dr. Susan Hassol, climate analyst and author.

Page 65 *The butterflies that disappeared couldn't survive* . . . : Fox, Richard. Butterfly Conservation Initiative. *Climate Change and Habitat Loss Hit Northern Butterflies.*; Franco, Aldina M. A., et al. "Impacts of Climate Warming and Habitat Loss on Extinctions at Species' Low-latitude Range Boundaries." *Global Change Biology* 12.8 (2006): 1545–53.

Page 66 *The red squirrel is literally being pushed* . . . : Egan, Timothy. "Heat Invades Cool Heights Over Arizona Desert." *The New York Times* 27 March 2007.

Page 67 *Some stronger butterflies* . . . : E-mail correspondence with Richard Fox, Surveys Manager, Butterfly Conservation Initiative.

Part Four: What You Can Do to Stop Global Warming

Page 70 . . . *the mayors of 418 cities:* www.sierraclub.org/coolcities.

Page 75 *If every kid in America* . . . : www.energystar.gov.

Page 75 *It would be like* . . . : www.energystar.gov/ia/partners/promotions/change_light/downloads/MayorToolkit.pdf.

Page 77 *Up to 10 percent* . . . : www.eia.doe.gov.

Page 78 *Americans use ten billion* . . . : American Forest and Paper Association. www.reusablebags.com/facts.php.

Page 80 *The more trees* . . . : Natural Resources Defense Council (NRDC). "Fact Sheet: Saving Paper in School."

Page 81 *Bringing in your own* . . . : Environmental Defense Fund.

Page 81 *Last year, one major* . . . : NRDC. *Nature's Voice.*

Page 81 *You want to buy* . . . : NRDC. "Environmentally Preferable Paper: Why and How to Buy It."

Page 81 *Forty percent of the fiber* . . . : Food and Agriculture Organization, FAOSTAT.

Page 81 *Fifteen trees are cut down* . . . : Conservatree. "Trees Into Paper." 2006. www.conservatree.com/learn/EnviroIssues/TreeStats.shtml.

Page 82 *Cars that sit* . . . : U.S. Environmental Protection Agency, Office of Mobile Sources: Fact Sheet OMS-18. "Your Car and Clean Air: What YOU Can Do to Reduce Pollution." August 1994. http://www.epa.gov/otaq/consumer/18-youdo.pdf.

Page 83 *The students of the University of Washington* . . . : Organic Consumers Association. www.organicconsumers.org/2006/article 1797.cfm.

Page 86 *A hybrid is high tech* . . . : NRDC. "Clean Air and Energy."

Page 87 *When combined with regular gasoline* . . . : "Waste-to-Energy Innovation." *WE Energies*. http://www.we-energies.com/environment/renewable_energy_biomass_tinedale.htm.

Page 88 *The Indy 500* . . . : www.indy500.com/news/story.php?story_id=4105.

Page 88 *An engine running on ethanol* . . . : Jones, Roland. "The Driver's Seat: Ethanol Boosters Hoping for Indy 500 Win." *MSNBC*. 28 May 2006. www.msnbc.msn.com/id/12740848.

Page 89 *Today, a typical wind turbine* . . . : Renewable Energy Systems. www.res-ltd.com/wind-power/faqs.htm.

Page 93 *Recent discoveries* . . . : Woodyard, Chris. "Honda Sees Possible Ethanol Breakthrough—New Microorganism Improves Efficiency." *USA Today* 15 September 2006.

Page 98 *The band Coldplay* . . . : Kher, Unmesh, et al. "How to Seize the Initiative." *Time* 3 April 2006, p. 46.

Page 99 *A company called Simple* . . . : Simple Shoe Company, "a nice little shoe company," www.simpleshoes.com, "Greentoeology," Spring 2007.

Page 99 *Kenny Luna* . . . : E-mail correspondence with Kenny Luna, eighth-grade teacher, at www.thebrightidea.blogspot.com.

Page 99 *Anne Lasker* . . . : Conversation with Anne Lasker, parent and creator of Trashion Show.

Selected Bibliography

Books

Dauncey, Guy, with Patrick Mazza. *Stormy Weather: 101 Solutions to Global Climate Change.* Gabriola Island, British Columbia, Canada: New Society Publishers, 2001.

Flannery, Tim. *The Weather Makers.* New York: Atlantic Monthly Press, 2005.

Gelbspan, Ross. *Boiling Point: How Politicians, Big Oil and Coal, Journalists and Activists Are Fueling the Climate Crisis—and What We Can Do to Avert Disaster.* New York: Basic Books, 2004.

Gore, Al. *An Inconvenient Truth.* New York: Rodale, 2006.

———. *Earth in the Balance: Ecology and the Human Spirit.* Boston: Houghton Mifflin, 2000.

Kolbert, Elizabeth. *Field Notes from a Catastrophe.* New York: Bloomsbury, 2006.

Tennesen, Michael. *The Complete Idiot's Guide to Global Warming.* New York: Alpha Publishing, 2004.

Tickell, Josh. *Biodiesel America: How to Achieve Energy Security, Free America from Middle-East Oil Dependence and Make Money Growing Fuel.* USA: Yorkshire Press, 2006.

Trask, Crissy. *It's Easy Being Green.* Layton, Utah: Gibbs Smith, 2006.

Magazines

BusinessWeek, Global Warming Issue, 16 August 2004.

The Economist, The Heat Is On Issue, September 9–15, 2006.

Mother Jones, As the World Burns Issue, June 2005.

National Geographic, Signs from Earth Issue, September 2004.

Natural History, Cooking the Climate with Coal Issue, May 2006.

Newsweek, Save the Planet — Or Else, 16 April 2007.

onearth, Natural Resources Defense Council magazine, various issues.

Time, Special Report: Global Warming Issue, 3 April 2006.

Time, The Global Warming Survival Guide, 9 April 2007.

Vanity Fair, Green Issue, May 2006.

Vanity Fair, Second Annual Green Issue, May 2007.

Articles and Reports

American Wind Energy Association. "Fact Sheet: Wind Power Today." 2004. www.awea.org.

Atkinson, Angus, et al. "Long-Term Decline in Antarctic Krill Stock and Increase in Salps Within the Southern Ocean." *Nature* 432.7013 (2004): 100–103.

Augustin, L. "New Evidence Extends Greenhouse Gas Record from Ice Cores by 50 Percent, Adding 210,000 Years." *Science* 25 November 2005.

Australian Academy of Science. "Biomass—the growing energy resource." www.science.org.au/nova/039.

Avant, Bill. "Paper or Plastic? A Simple Question, Right? Wrong!" *The Tennessee Conservationist.* January/February 2006. www.tn.gov/environment/tn_consv/archive/paperplastic.pdf.

British Antarctic Survey. *Oldest Antarctic Ice Core Reveals Climate History.* 09 June 2004 PR No. 7/2004.

Bryant, Dirk, et al. *The Last Frontier Forests: Ecosystems and economies on the edge.* Washington, D.C.: World Resources Institute, 1997.

Carey, John. "Business on a Warmer Planet." *BusinessWeek* 17 July 2006.

CNN: Science and Space, Associated Press. "Study: Earth Hottest in 400 years." 22 June 2006.

Connor, Steve. "Warmer Seas Will Wipe Out Plankton, Source of Ocean Life." *Independent News UK* 19 January 2006.

Conservatree. "Trees Into Paper." 2006. www.conservatree.com/learn/EnviroIssues/TreeStats.shtml.

Durner, George M., et al. "Predicting the Future Distribution of Polar Bear Habitat in the Polar Basin." U.S. Department of the Interior. U.S. Geological Survey.

Egan, Timothy. "Heat Invades Cool Heights Over Arizona Desert." *The New York Times* 27 March 2007.

Energy Information Administration. *Emissions of Greenhouse Gases in the United States, 2004.* Report #DOE/EIA 0573 (2004), December 2005.

Energy Quest. "Chapter 8: Fossil Fuels." http://www.energyquest.ca.gov/story/chapter08.html.

———. "Chapter 10: Biomass Energy." http://www.energyquest.ca.gov/story/chapter10.html.

———. "Chapter 11: Geothermal Energy." http://www.energyquest.ca.gov/story/chapter11.html.

———. "Chapter 12: Hydro Power." http://www.energyquest.ca.gov/story/chapter12.html.

Fialka, John J., and Kathryn Kranhold. "Lights Out for Old Bulbs?" *The Wall Street Journal* 13 September 2007.

Fox, Richard. Butterfly Conservation Initiative. *Climate Change and Habitat Loss Hit Northern Butterflies.*

Franco, Aldina M. A., et al. "Impacts of Climate Warming and Habitat Loss on Extinctions at Species' Low-latitude Range Boundaries." *Global Change Biology* 12.8 (2006): 1545–1553.

Heinz Center for Science, Economics, and the Environment. *Human Links to Coastal Disasters.* 2002.

Henne, Gudrun, and Christoph Thies. "Will the Last of the Ancient Forests Survive in 2050?" *Unasylva* 52.1 (2001).

"How Do Clouds Form?" *Forecasting the Weather Using Clouds.* 2001. http://snrs.unl.edu/amet351/noehrenberg/cloudformation.html.

Huisman, Jef, et al. Letter. "Reduced Mixing Generates Oscillations and Chaos in the Oceanic Deep Chlorophyll Maximum." *Nature* 439.4074 (2006): 322–325.

Intergovernmental Panel on Climate Change (IPCC). *Third Assessment Report: Climate Change 2001.*

———. *Fourth Assessment Report: Climate Change 2007: Summary for Policy Makers.*

Interstate Renewable Energy Council (IREC). *Schools Going Solar.* www.irecusa.org.

Jones, Roland. "The Driver's Seat: Ethanol Boosters Hoping for Indy 500 Win." *MSNBC.* 28 May 2006. www.msnbc.msn.com/id/12740848.

Kher, Unmesh, et al. "How to Seize the Initiative." *Time* 3 April 2006.

Malakunas, Karl. "Typhoon Saomai Kills Scores in China." *Discovery Channel: Discovery News.* 11 August 2006. http://dsc.discovery.com/news/2006/08/10/typhoon_pla.html?category=travel&guid=20060810100030.

Malcolm, Jay R., et al. "Global Warming and Extinctions of Endemic Species from Biodiversity Hotspots." *Conservation Biology* 20.2 (2006): 538–548.

Marshall, Gareth, et al. "The Impact of a Changing Southern Hemisphere Annular Mode on Antarctic Peninsula Summer Temperatures." *Journal of Climate* 19.20 (2006): 5388–5404.

McFarling, Usha Lee. "Altered Oceans: A Chemical Imbalance." *Los Angeles Times* 3 August 2006.

McGahee, Alvin L. National Oceanic Atmospheric Administration: National Climate Data Center (NCDC), United States Department of Commerce. *Selected U.S. City and State Extremes for July 2006.*

Mohan, Jacqueline E., et al. "Biomass and Toxicity Responses of Poison Ivy to Elevated Atmospheric

CO_2." *PNAS* 103.24 (2006): 9086–9089.

"NASA Survey Confirms Climate Warming Impact on Polar Ice Sheets: Release 06–089." National Aeronautic and Space Administration. 8 March 2006. http://www.nasa.gov/home/hqnews/2006/mar/HQ_06089_polar_ice_sheets_melting.html.

"National Assessment of Coastal Vulnerability to Future Sea Level Rise: Report Number 076-00." *U.S. Geological Survey.* June 2000. http://pubs.usgs.gov/fs/fs76-00/fs076-00.pdf.

Natural Resources Defense Council. "Hybrid Values." www.nrdc.org/air/transportation/ghybrid.asp.

———. "Environmentally Preferable Paper: Why and How to Buy It." *Paper Industry Reform Project,* January 2005.

———. "Fact Sheet: Saving Paper in School." www.nrdc.org/greensquad/library/paper.html.

———. *Nature's Voice.* January/February 2005.

New England Regional Assessment Group. *Preparing for a Changing Climate: The Potential Consequences of Climate Variability and Change.* New England Regional Overview, U.S. Global Change Research Program. University of New Hampshire, 2001.

"Ocean Acidification Due to Increasing Atmospheric Carbon Dioxide." *The Royal Society.* 30 June 2005.

Patz, Jonathan, et al. "Impact of Regional Climate Change on Human Health." *Nature* 438.7066 (2005): 310–317.

Poggioli, Sylvia. "Climate Change Threatens European Landmarks." *NPR Morning Edition* 17 August 2007.

Pounds, Alan, et al. "Widespread Amphibian Extinctions from Epidemic Disease Driven by Global Warming." *Nature* 439.7073 (2006): 161–167.

Ruttimann, Jacqueline. "Oceanography: Sick Seas." *Nature* 442.7106 (2006): 978–980.

Santer, B. D., et al. "Forced and Unforced Ocean Temperature Changes in Atlantic and Pacific Tropical Cyclogenesis Regions. *PNAS* 103.38 (2006): 13905–13910.

Saunders, Stephen, et al. "Losing Ground—Western National Parks Endangered by Climate Disruption." Rocky Mountain Climate Organization and Natural Resources Defense Council. July 2006.

Siegenthaler, Urs, et al. "Stable Carbon Cycle-Climate Relationship During the Late Pleistocene." *Science* 310 (2005): 1313–1317.

Stauth, David. "Global Warming Poses Risk to Pacific Northwest Snowpack, Ski Resorts." *Oregon State University News and Communications Services* 7 March 2006.

"Students recognized for outstanding energy projects." National Energy Education Development Project. 1 May 2007. http://www.need.org/needpdf/07pressindschool.pdf.

Tebaldi, Claudia, et al. "Going to the Extremes: An Intercomparison of Model-Simulated Historical and Future Changes in Extreme Events." *Climatic Change* 79.3/4 (2006): 185–211.

Texas A&M Student Counseling Services. "Top Jobs in Energy-Related Industries." www.scs.tamu.edu/articles/hotocs0805.asp.

Thomas, Chris D., et al. "Extinction Risk from Climate Change." *Nature* 427.6970 (2004): 145–147.

U.S. Environmental Protection Agency. "Drinking Water." www.epa.gov/region7/kids/drnk_b.htm.

———. "Recycling." http://www.epa.gov/epaoswer/non-hw/muncpl/recycle.htm.

———. "Conservation." www.epa.gov.

———. Office of Mobile Sources: Fact Sheet OMS-18. "Your Car and Clean Air: What YOU Can Do to Reduce Pollution." August 1994. http://www.epa.gov/otaq/consumer/18-youdo.pdf.

Van Voorhis, Scott. "Wally Would Be Proud as Fenway Park Goes Green." *Boston Herald* 21 September 2007.

"Waste-to-Energy Innovation." *WE Energies.* http://www.we-energies.com/environment/renewable_energy_biomass_tinedale.htm.

Westerling, A. L. "Warming and Earlier Spring Increase Western U.S. Forest Wildfire Activity." *Science* 313 (2006): 940–943.

Woodyard, Chris. "Honda Sees Possible Ethanol Breakthrough—New Microorganism Improves Efficiency." *USA Today* 15 September 2006.

Yeoman, Louise. "Venomous Snails Aid Medical Science." *BBC News Radio* 27 March 2006.

Ziska, L. H., et al. "Cities as harbingers of climate change: common ragweed, urbanization and public health." *Journal of Allergy Clinical Immunology* 111.2 (2003): 290–295.

Zwally, H. Jay, and Konrad Steffan. "Surface Melt-Induced Acceleration of Greenland Ice-Sheet Flow." *Science Express* 297 (2002): 218–212.

Web Sites

American Forest and Paper Association. www.afandpaorg.

Energy Star. www.energystar.gov/ia/partners/promotions/change_light/downloads/MayorToolkit.pdf.

Environmental Defense Fund. www.environmentaldefense.org.

Food and Agricultural Organization of the United Nations, FAOSTAT. www.faostat.fao.org.

Green dream jobs. www.sustainablebusiness.com/jobs.

Indianapolis 500. www.indy500.com/news/story.php?story_id=4105.

National Climatic Data Center (NCDC). www.ncdc.noaa.gov.

National Resources Defense Council (NRDC). www.nrdc.org.

The Nature Conservancy. www.nature.org.

The Nobel Prize. www.nobelprize.org.

Renewable Energy Access. www.renewableenergyaccess.com/rea/jobs/home.

Sierra Club. www.sierraclub.org.

U.S. Census Bureau, 2000. www.census.gov/population/www/socdemo/age.html.

U.S. Department of Energy. Energy Efficiency and Renewable Energy. www.fueleconomy.com.

———. Energy Efficiency and Renewable Energy, Alternative Fuels Data Center. www.eere.energy.gov.

———. Energy Information Agency. www.eia.doe.gov.

Renewable Energy Systems. www.res-ltd.com/wind-power/faqs.htm.

World Wildlife Fund. www.worldwildlife.org.

Interviews and Correspondence

Eric Chivian M.D., Director, Center for Health and the Global Environment, Harvard Medical School.

Dr. Heidi Cullen, The Weather Channel climate expert and host of *The Climate Code.*

Richard Fox, Surveys Manager, Butterfly Conservation Initiative.

Tim Greeff, Campaign Director, Natural Resources Defense Council Climate Center.

Dr. Susan Hassol, climate analyst and author.

Noah Horowitz, Senior Scientist, Natural Resources Defense Council.

Daniel A. Lashof, Ph.D., Science Director, Natural Resources Defense Council Climate Center.

Anne Lasker, parent and creator of Trashion Show.

Kenny Luna, eighth-grade teacher.

Dr. Gareth Marshall, climatologist, British Antarctic Survey.

Nigel Pervis, The Nature Conservancy.

Joel Reynolds, Director, Natural Resources Defense Council Marine Mammal Protection Program.

John Steelman, Campaign Director, Natural Resources Defense Council Climate Center.

Eric Wolff, British Antarctic Survey.

Photo Credits

Grateful acknowledgment is made for permission to reprint the following:

All illustrations, charts, and graphs by Stephen Schudlich.

Page iii, globe: NASA. *Page v, globe:* NASA. *Page vi, sky:* © Corbis Photography (RF)/Veer, CBP1001034. *Page viii, globe:* NASA; *compact fluorescent lightbulb:* © Albert Lozano/Shutterstock Inc., 1041557; *boy:* © Robert Recker/zefa/Corbis, 42-15289550. *Page ix, fall trees:* © AVTG/iStockphoto.com, 925210. *Pages xii–xiii, grass:* © jallfree/iStockphoto.com, 1933744.

Part 1

Pages 2–3, grass: © jallfree/iStockphoto.com, 1933744; *globe:* NASA; *blanketed chair:* © Johan Odmann/Johner Images/Getty Images, 72163467; *pizza:* © Vasko Miokovic/iStockphoto, 1933040. *Page 4, Whoopie Cushion:* © PunchStock, TOY04983-00; *cow:* © Joy Brown/Shutterstock Inc., 1881097. *Page 5, Popsicle:* © Kate Tero/iStockphoto 2004834. *Page 6, fossil:* © Dirk Wiersma/Photo Researchers Inc., SE8713. *Page 7, oil barrel:* © Michael Osterrieder/Shutterstock Inc., 2011086; *spark plug:* © ajt/Shutterstock Inc., 34807; *traffic:* © Steve Lovegrove/Shutterstock Inc., 555926. *Page 8, coal:* © Sally Wallis/Shutterstock Inc., 1758426; *flames:* © J. Helgason/Shutterstock Inc., 1026956; *city lights:* © Carlos Sanchez Pereyra/Shutterstock Inc., 1026956; *pipeline:* © Reed Kaestner/ Corbis RF/SCHL, CB023359; *match:* © William Mahnken/Shutterstock Inc., 500119; *snowy house:* © Carsten Madsen/iStockphoto.com 1402087. *Page 9, coal miner:* © Tyler Stableford/Stone/Getty Images, 200438538-001. *Page 10, smokestacks:* © Steve Cole/Photodisc Green (RF)/Getty Images, BU005598. *Page 11, steam engine:* © Michael DiMunno/Shutterstock Inc., 62546. *Pages 12–13, surfer:* © Joe Mcbride/Photographer's Choice/Getty Images, 200350671-002; *Page 15, tree:* © Martin Rueger/Image Bank/Getty Images, 200332564-001. *Page 16, Dome C overview:* Courtesy British Antarctic Survey. *Page 17, Dome C ice core:* Courtesy Chris Gilbert/British Antarctic Survey. *Page 19, iceberg:* © Frank Krahmer /Masterfile, 700-00557458; *The Wicked Witch:* THE WIZARD OF OZ © Turner Entertainment Co. A Warner Bros. Entertainment Company. All Rights Reserved. *Page 20, Polar ice cap:* NASA, Goddard Space Flight Center, Scientific Visualization Studio. *Page 21, permafrost:* W. K. Fletcher/Photo Researchers Inc., BC6337. *Page 22, clear-cut mountain:* © Art Twomey/Photo Researchers Inc., 6V4711. *Page 23, Will Ferrell:* Courtesy BWR Public Relations; *piggy bank:* © Boden/Ledingham/Masterfile, 700-00318694. *Pages 24–25, sea:* © Stockbyte (RF)/Getty Images, dv030411; *SpongeBob SquarePants:* © 2006 Viacom International Inc. All rights reserved. Nickelodeon, SpongeBob SquarePants and all related titles, logos and characters are trademarks of Viacom International Inc. "SpongeBob SquarePants" created by Stephen Hillenburg. *Page 26, footprint:* © James Levin, DSC_3661. *Page 29 A, Reggie Bush:* © Sean Gardner/Reuters/Corbis, 42-17737181; *B, Jennifer Garner:* © Sheryl Nields/Icon International (photo provided by Management 360); *C, Shaun White:* © Bo Bridges/Corbis, 42-17259751; *D, Sheryl Crow:* Courtesy Chris Hudson; *E, Jim Lovell:* © Bettmann/Corbis, U1658271; *F, Leonardo DiCaprio:* © AP Photo/Kevork Djansezian, 04120207325; *G, Cedric the Entertainer:* © Don Tucci/Courtesy Entertainment Enterprises; *H, Laird Hamilton:* © Tony Friedkin/Sony Pictures Classics/ Zuma/Corbis, DWF15-575953.

Part 2

Page 32, muscle: © Tomasz Trojanowski/Shutterstock Inc., 2649385; *satellite view of Hurricane Katrina:* NOAA. *Page 33, Category 1 hurricane:* Courtesy PDPhoto.org, Waves 2002012014; *Category 3 hurricane:* Courtesy Jeff Williams/morgueFile.com, 85453; *Category 5 hurricane:* Courtesy Craig Toocheck/stock.xchng, 502911. *Page 34, cows:* FEMA News Photo/G. Mathieson, 314. *Page 35, typhoon:* © JTB Photo/Photolibrary, 141602129D. *Page 36, flooding:* © Royalty-Free/Corbis, CB031981. *Page 38, dry riverbed:* © Christopher J. Morris/Corbis, AAFR001149. *Page 39, dry, cracked earth:* © 2007 Gary Braasch/ILCP; *Map:* Jim McMahon/Scholastic. *Page 40, cornfield afflicted by drought:* © JP Laffont/Sygma/Corbis, 42-16984834. *Page 41, X-Games cyclist:* © Phil Ellsworth/ESPN. *Page 42, heat-exhausted dogs:* © BIOS Balcaen Claude/Peter Arnold Inc., 108415. *Page 43, spectators sprayed with water:* © Snaps/Action Press/Zuma/Newscom, zumaphotos 469368. *Page 44, abandoned beach house:* © 2007 Gary Braasch/ILCP. *Page 45, Tuvalu wave:* © 2007 Gary Braasch/ILCP. *Pages 46–47, Mt. Rainier:* © J. A. Kraulis/Masterfile, 700-00033972. *Pages 48–49, grass:* © jallfree/iStockphoto.com, 1933744; *poison ivy:* © Keith Spieldenner/Shutterstock Inc., 819211; *fall leaf:* © Tobias Machhaus/Shutterstock Inc., 2229998; *skier:* © Geir Olav Lyngfjell/Shutterstock Inc., 2821663; *ragweed:* © Steve Cole/Masterfile, 700-00193971; *hockey players:* © Photodisc (RF)/Getty Images, rbs1_54; *mosquito:* © 3D4Medical.com/Getty Images, 73337318; *bark beetle:* © Rod Planck/Photo Researchers Inc., 6Y6488; *pancakes:* © bluestocking/Shutterstock Inc., 2800454.

Part 3

Page 53, Map: Jim McMahon/Scholastic. *Page 54, walrus:* © Kevin Schafer/ILCP, 153181. *Page 55, emperor penguin:* © Kevin Schafer/ILCP, 121329; *dead polar bear:* © Doug Allan/Oxford Scientific/Photolibrary, OSF 20035979; *polar bears:* © Kevin Schafer/ILCP, 110459. *Page 56, polar bear:* © Wayne Bilenduke/The Image Bank/Getty Images, 200121503-001. *Page 58, blue whale:* © Francois Gohier/Photo Researchers Inc., BD8807. *Page 59, healthy coral:* © Darryl Leniuk/Masterfile, 700-00623405. *Page 60, bleached coral:* Courtesy Ray Berkelmans, Australian Institute of Marine Science. *Page 61, bleached coral:* Courtesy Ray Berkelmans, Australian Institute of Marine Science. *Page 62, Monteverde Cloud Forest:* © Kevin Schafer/Peter Arnold Inc. PA0071639; *golden toad:* Charles H. Smith/U.S. Fish and Wildlife Service, source #WO-2691-13. *Page 64, monarch butterfly:* © Royalty-Free/Masterfile, 616-00413874. *Page 65, Scotch Argus Butterfly:* © Laurie Campbell/NHPA, 00014702; *Ringlet butterfly:* © Sergey Chushkin/Shutterstock Inc., 1133407. *Page 66, Mt. Graham red squirrel:* © John Cancalosi/Peter Arnold Inc., PA1242871.

Part 4

Pages 70–71, U.S. Capitol Building: © Randy Wells/Stone/Getty Images, 454610-001. *Page 72, Portland bike lane:* © Jonathan Maus/BikePortland.org, DSC_1910. *Page 74, compact fluorescent lightbulb:* © Albert Lozano/Shutterstock Inc., 1041557; *girl:* © Steve Craft/Iconica/Getty Images, 200348188-002. *Page 76, wall with outlet:* © Creasence/Shutterstock Inc., 2915616; *Energy Star logo:* Courtesy Energy Star, U.S. Environmental Protection Agency. *Page 77, plugs with cords:* Anthony Berenyi/Shutterstock Inc., 2616366. *Page 78, paper bag:* © Photos.com, 8020375; *plastic bag:* © Stephen Stickler/Photographer's Choice/Getty Images, 200470838-001; *canvas bag:* © James Levin, DSC_4013. *Page 80, Muir Woods:* Walter Meayers Edwards/National Geographic/Getty Images, ngs0_8548. *Pages 82–83, sky:* © Corbis Photography (RF)/Veer, CBP1001034; *notepaper:* © Siede Preis/Photodisc (RF)/Getty Images, AA003104. *Page 84, sky:* © Corbis Photography (RF)/Veer, CBP1001034; *notepaper:* © Siede Preis/Photodisc (RF)/Getty Images, AA003104; *classroom:* © Stockbyte Photography (RF)/Veer, SBP0353011. *Page 85, school with solar panels:* Courtesy Glen Kizer for Foundation for Environmental Education. *Page 86, NYC city bus:* Courtesy Ernie Mauro, BAE Systems; *Prius:* Courtesy, © 2007 Toyota Motor Sales, U.S.A., INC. *Page 87, wheat field:* © Harald Sund/Photographer's Choice/Getty Images, 200364465-001; *flex-fuel car:* Josiah Cuneo/Courtesy greasecar.com. *Page 88, Indy 500:* Courtesy Indy Racing League, indycar.com, photographer Chris Jones. *Page 89, wind turbine farm:* © Rafa Irusta/Shutterstock Inc., 1242320. *Page 90, Dell-Winston solar car:* Courtesy Dell-Winston School Solar Car Challenge. *Page 91, Old Faithful:* © Emanuele Taroni/ Photodisc (RF)/Getty Images, AA019665. *Page 92, Grand Coulee Dam:* © Philip Gendreau/Bettmann/Corbis, GNGN388. *Page 93, wood chips:* © Elena Elisseeva/Shutterstock Inc., 3039011. *Pages 94–95, sky:* © Corbis Photography (RF)/Veer, CBP1001034. *Page 96, sky:* © Corbis Photography (RF)/Veer, CBP1001034; *Gro Harlem Brundtland:* © Ralph Orlowski/Getty Images, 52193186. *Page 97, Eagles logo:* Courtesy Philadelphia Eagles; *Paul Frank logo:* Courtesy Paul Frank; *Ugg logo:* Courtesy Ugg Austrailia; *MTV logo:* Courtesy thinkmtv. *Page 98, Coldplay:* © Kevin Westenberg/Courtesy 3 D Management. *Page 99, globe:* NASA.

Pages 100–101, grass: © jallfree/iStockphoto.com, 1933744. *Page 102, Stopglobalwarming.org logo:* Courtesy Laurie David and The Tide Center. *Page 112, sky:* © Corbis Photography (RF)/Veer, CBP1001034; *authors:* Stacie Isabella Turk, Ribbonhead. *Page 113, sky:* © Corbis Photography (RF)/Veer, CBP1001034. *Page 114, Stopglobalwarming.org logo:* Courtesy Laurie David and The Tide Center.

Index

*Page numbers in **boldface** refer to photographs.*

About the Authors

Laurie David is a global warming activist and the producer of the Academy Award-winning film *An Inconvenient Truth* and the HBO documentary *Too Hot Not to Handle*. She executive-produced *Earth to America!,* a primetime comedy special about global warming, which earned her a Gracie Allen Award for Individual Achievement. A trustee of the Natural Resources Defense Council, Laurie founded the Stop Global Warming Virtual March with Senator John McCain and Robert F. Kennedy, Jr. She was the first-ever guest editor of the green May 2006 and 2007 issues of *Elle* magazine. In 2006 Laurie published her first book, the bestseller *Stop Global Warming: The Solution Is You*. She also launched the Stop Global Warming College Tour with Sheryl Crow, on which they visited college campuses throughout the Southeast on a biodiesel tour bus.

Laurie David received the prestigious Stanley Kramer Award from the Producers Guild of America and a Humanitas Prize Special Award for *An Inconvenient Truth*. She has been honored with the Audubon Society's Rachel Carson Award, the Feminist Majority's Eleanor Roosevelt Award, the NRDC's 2006 Forces for Nature Award, and by Robert F. Kennedy Jr.'s Riverkeeper organization.

Laurie, a regular blogger on the Huffington Post, has been featured on such shows as *Oprah*, *Good Morning America*, and on CNN and has been profiled in numerous magazines, including *Vanity Fair*, which called her the "Bono of climate change." She lives in Los Angeles, California.

Cambria Gordon is an award-winning former advertising copywriter who now pursues children's writing full-time. Her credits include a nonfiction book, *Fifty Nifty Crafts to Make With Things Around the House*, and an episode for the award-winning animated Disney Channel series *Madeline*.

Cambria is an active environmentalist and lives with her husband and their three children in Los Angeles, California.

stopglobalwarming.org